meditation for
busy people

OSHO

meditation for busy people

Stress-beating strategies to calm your life

St. Martin's Griffin ♏ New York

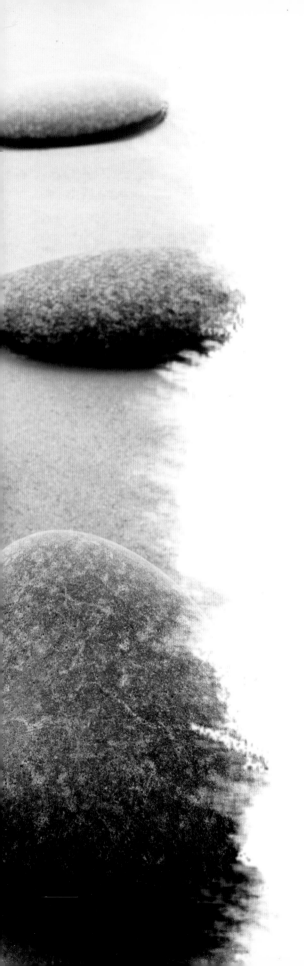

Library of Congress Cataloging-in-Publication Data Available Upon Request

ISBN 0-312-34302-7
EAN 978-0312-34302-6

First published in Great Britain by Hamlyn, a division of Octopus Publishing
Group, Ltd

First U.S. Edition: May 2005

10 9 8 7 6 5 4 3 2 1

contents

part one

understanding the roots of stress

Tension has nothing to do with anything outside you, it is to do with what is happening within you. You will always find an external excuse to rationalize your tension simply because it looks so idiotic to be tense without any reason.
But tension is not outside you; it lies in your incorrect lifestyle. You are always thinking either of the past or of the future and missing the present, which is the only reality — that will create tension.

lighting up the inner

Wisdom is not the accumulation of facts, figures and information – it is a transformation of your inner space.

We are living outside ourselves, hence our inner world remains dark. If we turn in, if our attention starts focusing inwards, then light is created. We have everything that is needed to create light; it is simply that a rearrangement is needed.

It is as if somebody has messed up your room – the furniture is upside-down, the chandelier is on the floor. Everything is there but not in its place. It is difficult to live in such a room. You will have to put things back exactly where they belong.

This is how the human being is: we have everything that is needed, existence has provided everything. We come absolutely ready to live our lives to the optimum, but we live at the minimum for the simple reason that we never arrange things. For example, our attention is directed outwards, hence we can see everybody except ourselves – and that is the most important thing to see. It is perfectly good to see others, but first you have to see yourself, first you have to be yourself. From that vantage point, from that centred state, you can look at others and that will give you a totally different quality.

So the attention has to be turned inwards. That's what self-discovery is all about – a 180-degree turn of our attentiveness, of our awareness. And wherever we focus our awareness, that space becomes lit up. I am not against the outside world but the inside world is the first to be taken care of, and the outside world takes second place. The person who can take care of his or her inner world is easily capable of taking care of the outside world.

Wisdom means knowing oneself, and to know oneself is the beginning of all other knowing. Then the circle of your light can go on spreading; it can become more and more comprehensive. A moment comes when your wisdom comprehends everything, it becomes all-inclusive. When one feels nothing is missing, nothing is lacking, one has come home. There is great relaxation, rest, fulfilment, deep contentment; there is a silence, yet it is full of songs.

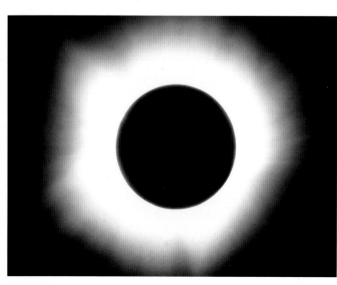

...if our attention starts focusing inwards, then light is created.

the pathology of ambition

all cultures and all religions condition you to feel negative about yourself. Nobody is loved or appreciated for just being him or herself. You are asked to prove whether you are of any worth: bring gold medals from the sports field, achieve success, money, power, prestige, respectability. Prove yourself! Your worth is not intrinsic; that's what you have been taught. Your worth has to be proved.

Hence a deep antagonism towards oneself arises, a deep feeling that 'I am worthless as I am – unless proved otherwise.' Very few people can succeed in this competitive world. Millions and millions of people are competing – how many can succeed? How many people can become presidents and prime ministers? In a country of millions, only one person will become the president, but deep down everybody hankers for the job. Millions will feel that they are unworthy. How many people can become great painters? Yet everybody has something to create. How many people can become great poets like Shakespeare, Milton or Shelley? Yet everybody has something of the poetic in their innermost being; everybody has some poetry to give to the world. But when it becomes an ambition, ambition in itself is anti-poetic.

The idea of success is torturing you. It is the greatest calamity that has happened to humanity: the idea of success, that you have

to 'succeed'. And success means you have to compete, you have to fight – by fair means or foul, it doesn't matter. Once you succeed, everything is okay. The key point is success; even if by foul means you succeed, once you are successful, whatever you have done is acceptable.

Success changes the quality of all your acts. Success changes evil means into good ones. So the only question is, how to succeed, how to reach the top? And naturally, very few people can reach the top. If everybody is trying to reach Everest, how many people can stand there? There is not much space at the peak; only one person can be there with ease. The millions who were also striving will feel like failures and a great despair will settle in their souls. They will start feeling negative.

This is a wrong kind of education. It is utterly poisonous, this so-called education that has been given to you. Your schools and colleges, your universities are poisoning you. They are creating misery for you; they are the places where hells are manufactured – but in such a beautiful way that you never become aware of what is going on. The whole world has become a hell because of wrong education. Any education that is based on the idea of ambition is going to create hell on earth – and it has succeeded.

Everybody is suffering and feeling inferior. This is really a strange situation. Nobody is inferior and nobody is superior, because each

individual is unique – no comparison is possible. You are you, and you are simply you, and you cannot be anybody else. And there is no need, either. You need not become famous, you need not be a success in the eyes of the world. These are all foolish ideas.

All that you need is to be creative, loving, aware, meditative ... if you feel poetry arising in you, write it for yourself, for your husband, for your children, for your friends – and forget all about it! Sing your song, and if nobody listens, sing it alone and enjoy it! Go to the trees and they will applaud and appreciate it. Or talk to the birds and the animals, and they will understand far more than human beings that have been poisoned for centuries and centuries with wrong concepts of life.

The ambitious person is pathological.

You feel negative about yourself because that's how you have been made to feel. Your parents have done it to you – this is your heritage. Your teachers have done it to you, your religious leaders have too. Your political leaders have done it to you – and so many people are doing it that, naturally, you have accepted the very idea that you are worthless, that you don't have any intrinsic meaning or value, that you don't have any significance of your own.

Each parent is saying to each child, 'Prove that you have some worth!' Being, just being, is not enough – some doing is needed.

My whole approach is that being is intrinsically valuable. Just that you are is such a gift from existence, what more can you ask for? Just to breathe in this beautiful existence is proof enough that existence loves you, that it needs you; otherwise you would not be here. You are! Existence has given birth to you. There must have been an immense need and you have filled a gap. Without you, existence would be less. And when I say this, I am saying it not only to you: I am saying it to the trees, to the birds, to the animals, to the pebbles on the shore. A single pebble less on the immense seashore and the seashore would not be the same. A single flower less and the universe would miss it.

You have to learn that you are valuable as you are. And I am not teaching you to be egotistical – quite the contrary. If you feel that you are valuable as you are, you will also feel that others are valuable as they are.

Accept people as they are; drop 'shoulds' and 'oughts' – these are enemies. People are carrying so many 'shoulds': 'do this and don't do that!'. You are carrying so many dos and don'ts that you cannot dance; the burden is too heavy. You have been given so many ideals and goals – ideals of perfection – that you always feel you are falling short. And the ideals are utterly impossible to achieve. You cannot fulfil them; there is no possibility of fulfilling them. So you will always fall short.

To be a perfectionist is to be ready for the psychiatrist's couch; to be a perfectionist is to be a neurotic. And we have all been told to be perfect.

Life is beautiful in all its imperfections. Nothing is perfect. Let me say to you: even God is not perfect – because if God is perfect then

Friedrich Nietzsche is right that God is dead. Perfection means death! Perfection means there is no possibility of further growth. Perfection means now everything is finished. Imperfection means it is possible to grow. Imperfection means the excitement of new pastures, ecstasy, adventure. Imperfection means that you are alive, that life is going to continue.

Life is eternal, hence I say life is eternally imperfect. There is nothing wrong in being imperfect. Accept your imperfection and then the idea of being negative towards yourself will disappear. Accept your present state and don't compare it with some future perfection, future ideal. Don't think in terms of how you should be! That is the root of all pathology – drop that. You are as you are today, and tomorrow you may be different. But you cannot predict it today, and there is no need to plan for it either.

Live this day in all its beauty, in all its joy, in all its pain, agony, ecstasy. Live it in its

Live this day in all its beauty, in all its joy, in all its pain...

totality – in its darkness, in its light. Live the hate and live the love. Live the anger and live the compassion. Live whatever exists at this moment.

My approach is not that of perfection but that of totality. Live the moment that is available to you totally and the next moment will be born out of it. If this moment has been lived totally, the next is going to reach a higher pitch of totality, a higher peak of totality – because from where is the next moment going to come? It is going to be born out of this moment. Forget all about the future – the present is enough.

Jesus says, 'Think not of the morrow, and look at the lilies in the field! How beautiful they are. Even Solomon was not so beautiful attired in all his grandeur.' And what is the secret of the beautiful lilies? The secret is simple: they think not of the morrow, they don't know anything of the future. Tomorrow exists not. This day is enough unto itself; this moment is enough unto itself. And your feeling of negativity about yourself will disappear.

Remember, if you feel negative about yourself, you will automatically feel negative about others. That is a necessary corollary. It has to be understood. The person who is negative about himself cannot be positive about anybody else either, because the faults

that he finds in himself he will find in others – in fact he will magnify them in others. He will take revenge. Your parents have made you negative about yourself and you will take revenge on your children; you will make them even more negative.

Hence, negativity goes on growing with each generation. Each generation becomes more and more pathological. If modern people are suffering so much psychologically, it has nothing to do with the people themselves; it simply shows that the whole past has been wrong. It is the accumulation of the whole past. Unless we drop this whole pathological past and start anew, living in the present, with no idea of perfection, with no ideals, with no 'shoulds', with no commandments, humanity is doomed.

Everybody is feeling negative. One may say it, one may not say it. And when one feels negative about oneself, one feels negative about everything else. One's attitude becomes negative, that of 'no'. And if a negative person is taken to the rosebush she will count the thorns rather than look at the rose flower – she cannot. She is not capable of that. She will simply ignore the rose flower and will count the thorns.

If you are feeling negative, then the whole of life becomes a dark night. There are no

...Live it in its totality — in its darkness, in its light.

more dawns, the mornings are never there. The sun only sets and never rises. Your dark nights are not even full of stars. What can you say about stars? You don't even have a small candle.

The negative person lives in darkness, lives a kind of death. He slowly dies. That's what he thinks life is. He goes on poisoning himself in many ways; he is self-destructive. And, naturally, whoever comes in contact with him, he destroys that person too. A negative mother will destroy the child. The negative husband will destroy the wife; the negative wife will destroy the husband. The negative parents will destroy their children; the negative teacher will destroy her students.

A new humanity is needed that will affirm life, that will love life, that will love love, that will love this existence as it is, that will not make demands that first it has to be perfect, that will celebrate life with all its limitations. And you will be surprised – if you love your life, life starts opening its doors to you. If you love, mysteries are revealed to you, secrets are handed over to you. If you love your body, sooner or later you will become aware of the soul that resides in it. If you love the trees and the mountains and the rivers, sooner or later you will see the invisible hands of God behind everything. His signature is on every leaf. You just need eyes to see – and only positive eyes can see; negative eyes cannot see.

Accept yourself, otherwise you will become a hypocrite. And what is a hypocrite? The person who says one thing, believes one thing, and lives quite the contrary. Don't repress anything – nothing is negative in you. Existence is utterly positive. Express your hiddenmost core. Sing your song, and don't be worried what it is. Don't expect anybody to applaud it, there is no need. Singing in itself should be the reward.

If you want to really live, you will need a deep 'yes' in your heart. It is only 'yes' that allows you to live. It gives you nourishment, it gives you space to move. Just watch – even when repeating the word 'yes', something starts opening up in you. Say 'no', and something shrinks. Say no, repeat no, and you are killing yourself. Say yes and you will feel overflowing. Say yes and you are ready to love, to live, to be.

To me, each individual is superb, unique. I don't compare individuals; comparison is not my way, because comparison is always ugly and violent. I will not say you are superior to others, I will not say you are inferior to anybody. You are just yourself, and you are needed as you are. And you are incomparable – as everybody else is.

part two

part two

making the body-mind connection

Why do people look so tired? They are all fighting. Your religion teaches you to fight – your whole upbringing is based on conflict, because it is only through struggle that the ego can be created. When you relax, the ego disappears. To relax means to become egoless. If you go with the river, you cannot create an ego. The ego is an unnatural phenomenon; it needs great energy to create it and it needs great energy to maintain it. It is a very expensive phenomenon to have an ego. Your whole life is wasted on it.

awareness and relaxation: two sides of the same coin

Why are you tense? Your identification with all kinds of thoughts and fears – death, bankruptcy, the dollar going down ... these are your tensions, and they affect your body too. Your body also becomes tense, because body and mind are not two separate entities. Body-mind is a single system, so when the mind becomes tense, the body becomes tense.

Awareness and relaxation are two sides of the same coin. You cannot separate them. You can begin with awareness, and then you will find yourself relaxing...

Awareness takes you away from the mind and the identifications of the mind. Naturally, the body starts relaxing. You are no longer attached, and tensions cannot exist in the light of awareness.

You can start from the other end also. Just relax ... let all tensions drop ... and as you relax you will be surprised that a certain awareness is arising in you. But to start from awareness is easier; to start with relaxation is a little difficult, because even the effort to relax creates a certain tension.

There is an American book called *You Must Relax*. Now if the must is there, how can you relax? The must will make you tense; the very word immediately creates tension. 'Must' comes like a commandment from God. Perhaps the person who wrote the book knows nothing about relaxation and knows nothing about the complexities of relaxation.

Hence in the East, we have never started meditation from relaxation; we have started meditation from awareness. Then relaxation comes of its own accord; you don't have to bring it. If you have to bring it, there will be a certain tension. It should come on its own; only then will it be pure relaxation. And it comes.

If you want to, you can try to start from relaxation, but not with any idea of 'must'. To begin with relaxation is difficult, but if you want to try, I have an idea of how you should start. I have been working with many Western people and I have become aware of the fact that they don't belong to the East and they don't know the Eastern current of consciousness; they are coming from a different tradition that has never known any awareness.

For Western people especially, I have created meditations like Dynamic Meditation. While I was conducting camps of meditators I used a gibberish meditation, and the Kundalini Meditation. If you want to start from relaxation, then these meditations have to be done first. They will take out all the tensions from your mind and body, and then relaxation is very easy. You don't know how much you are holding in, and that this is the cause of tension.

I allowed gibberish meditation in the camps in the mountains. It is difficult to allow it in the city, because the neighbours go crazy. They start phoning the police and saying, 'Our whole life is being destroyed!' They don't know that if they participated in their own houses, they would be released from the insanity in which they are living! But they are not even aware of their insanity.

During the gibberish meditation, everybody was allowed to say aloud whatever came into his or her mind. It was such a joy to hear what people were saying – irrelevant, absurd – because I was the only witness. You could do whatever you wanted and the only condition was that you should not touch anybody else. People were doing all kinds of things ... somebody was standing on his head, somebody else had thrown off his clothes and ran around naked – for the whole hour!

One man used to sit every day in front of me – he must have been a broker or

From unawareness to awareness is the greatest quantum leap...

something similar – and as the meditation began, first he would smile, just at the idea of what he was going to do. Then he would pick up his phone, 'Hello, hello... ' He would go on looking at me out of the corner of his eye. I would avoid looking at him so as not to disturb his meditation. He was selling his shares, purchasing – he spent the whole hour on the phone.

Everybody was doing all the strange things that they had been holding back. When the meditation ended there was a ten-minute relaxation period, and in those ten minutes people lay down, not through any conscious decision, but because they were utterly exhausted. All the rubbish had been thrown out, so they felt a certain cleanliness and they relaxed. Thousands of people lying down silently ... and you would not think that even a thousand people were there.

People used to come to me and say, 'Prolong those ten minutes, because in our whole lives we have never experienced such relaxation, such joy. We had never thought we would ever understand what awareness is, but then we felt it was coming.'

So if you want to start with relaxation, first you have to go through a cathartic process: Dynamic Meditation, Kundalini or gibberish.

You may not know the origin of the word gibberish; it comes from a Sufi mystic whose name was Jabbar – and that was his only meditation. Whenever someone came, he would say, 'Sit down and start' – and people knew what he meant. He never talked, he never gave any discourses; he simply taught people gibberish. For example, once in a while he would give a demonstration. For half an hour he would talk all kinds of nonsense in a made-up language; he said just whatever came into his mind. That was his only teaching – and to those who had understood it, he would simply say, 'Sit down and start'.

Jabbar helped many people to become completely silent. How long can you go on talking? Eventually the mind becomes empty. Slowly, slowly a deep nothingness arises ... and in that nothingness a flame of awareness. It is always present, surrounded by your gibberish. The gibberish has to be taken out; that is your poison.

The same is true about the body. Your body has tensions. Just start making any movements that the body wants to make. You should not manipulate it. If it wants to dance, it wants to jog, it wants to run, it wants to roll around on the ground, you should not do it, you should simply allow it. Tell the body, 'You are free, do whatever you want' – and you will be surprised. 'My God! All these things the body wanted to do but I was holding back, and that was the tension.'

So there are two kinds of tension, the body tensions and the mind tensions. Both have to be released before you can start relaxation, which will bring you to awareness.

But beginning from awareness is far easier, and particularly for those who can understand the process of awareness, which is very simple. All day long you use your awareness with things – cars, traffic – even in the traffic you survive! It is absolutely mad. You are using awareness without being aware of it, but only with outside things. It is the same awareness that has to be used for the inside traffic. When you close your eyes there is a traffic of thoughts, emotions, dreams, imaginations; all kinds of things start flashing by.

What you have been doing in the outside world, do exactly the same with the inside world and you will become a witness. And once tasted, the joy of being a witness is so great, so otherworldly, that you would like to go more and more in. Whenever you find time, you would like to go more and more into your inner world.

It is not a question of any posture; it is not a question of any temple, of any church or synagogue. Sitting in a bus or in a railway carriage, when you have nothing to do, just close your eyes. It will keep your eyes from becoming tired of looking outside, and it will give you time enough to watch yourself. Those moments will become moments of the most beautiful experiences.

And slowly, slowly, as awareness grows, your whole personality starts changing. From unawareness to awareness is the greatest quantum leap.

Just learn to be aware in all situations. Make a point of using every situation for developing awareness.

don't try harder

more energy is needed to be miserable than to be blissful. Blissfulness is a state of nature – in fact, no energy is needed to be blissful because it is natural. Energy is needed to be miserable because it is unnatural. The more natural you are, the less energy is needed; the more unnatural you want to be, the more energy will be needed.

If you are standing on your feet, you need less energy; try to stand on your head and you need more energy. Whenever you see that more energy is needed, you will know that you are trying to do something unnatural. Meditation requires no energy because meditation is passive, inactive, silent. You are not doing anything – why should you need any energy?

Anger needs energy, thinking needs energy, violence needs energy – because you are doing something against nature, you are fighting against nature. It is like trying to swim upstream. If you are going with the river, then no energy is needed. The river takes you. But if you are trying to go upstream, then great energy will be needed – because you will be fighting against the stream.

Why do people look so tired? They are all fighting. Your religion teaches you to fight, your whole upbringing is based on conflict, because it is only through fight that the ego can be created. When you relax, the ego

...no energy is needed to be blissful because it is natural

disappears. To relax means to become egoless. If you go with the river, you cannot create the ego. The ego is an unnatural phenomenon; it needs great energy to create it and it needs great energy to maintain it. It is a very expensive phenomenon to have an ego. Your whole life is wasted in it.

The first thing I would like to tell you is that awareness does not need energy. You will be surprised: unawareness needs energy. Meditation does not need energy; thinking needs energy. Relaxation needs no energy! Tension needs energy, anxiety needs energy.

So don't miss the point. It is not a question of making an effort to be aware. If you make an effort, you will create tensions inside yourself – all effort brings tensions. If you try to be aware, you are fighting with yourself. There is no need to fight. Awareness is not a by-product of effort; awareness is a fragrance of let-go. Awareness is a flowering of surrender, of relaxation.

Just sit silently in a relaxed state, doing nothing ... and awareness will start happening. You don't have to pull it up from somewhere, you don't have to bring it from somewhere. It will shower on you from nowhere. You just be silent, sitting, and it will well up from within your own sources.

I understand that it is very difficult to sit silently; thoughts keep on coming. So let them come! Don't fight with your thoughts and you will not need any energy. Just allow

them to come – what else can you do? Clouds come and clouds go; let the thoughts come and let them go whenever they want to. Don't be on guard, and don't take the attitude that thoughts should come or should not come – don't be judgemental. Let them come, and let them go. Let yourself be utterly empty. Thoughts will pass, they will come and go, and slowly you will see that you remain unaffected by their coming and going. And when you are unaffected by their coming and going, they start disappearing, they evaporate ... Not by your effort but by your cool, calm emptiness, your relaxed state.

And don't feel that that relaxation will need great energy. How can relaxation need energy? Relaxation simply means you are not doing anything.

Sitting silently,
Doing nothing,
The spring comes
And the grass grows by itself...

Let this mantra sink into your heart. This is the very essence of meditation – Sitting silently ... doing nothing ... the spring comes ... and the grass grows by itself... Everything happens! You are not to be a doer.

Don't make awareness your goal, otherwise you have missed my point.

When the time comes, when the spring comes, the grass grows of its own accord. You need not pull the grass from the earth. All you have to do is learn the ways of relaxation and let go.

don't choose

the moment you choose, you are no longer whole; something has been rejected, something has been chosen. You have taken a side; you are for something, against something else. You are no longer whole; you are divided.

You say, 'I choose meditation, and I am not going to be angry any more.' Misery is bound to be the result. Meditation will not happen, only misery will happen! In the name of meditation now you will be miserable – and one can find beautiful names for one's misery.

Choosing itself is misery. To be choiceless is to be blissful. See it! Look into it as deeply as possible, and see that choosing itself is misery. Even if you choose bliss, misery will be created. Don't choose at all, and then see what happens.

It is very difficult not to choose. We have always been choosing; our whole life has been a series of choices. We have believed that unless we choose, who is going to choose for us? Unless we decide, who is going to decide for us? Unless we fight, who is going

Existence is our home; we belong to it, it belongs to us...

to fight for us? We have believed in a very stupid notion: that existence is against us, that we have to fight, that we have to be constantly on guard against existence.

Existence is not against you. You are just a ripple in this ocean – you are not separate from existence. How can existence be against you? You are part of it! It is existence that has given birth to you – how can the mother be against the child?

Existence is our home; we belong to it, it belongs to us. So there is no need to be worried, and there is no need to fight for private ends and private goals. One can relax with it – in the sun, in the wind, in the rain. One can relax with it. The sun is part of us as we are part of the sun; and the trees are part of us as we are part of the trees. Just see that the whole of existence is interdependent; it is a tremendously complicated network, but everything is joined with everything else. Nothing is separate. So what is the point of choosing? Simply live whatever you are, in your totality.

A problem arises because you will find polar opposites inside you, and the logical mind says, 'How can I be both?' Somebody once asked me: 'Whenever I am in love, meditation is disturbed. Whenever I meditate, I start losing my interest in love. So what should I do? What should I choose?'

The idea of choice arises because there are polarities. Yes, it is true: if you fall in love you will tend to forget about meditation and if you go into meditation, you will lose interest in love. But still there is no need to choose! When you feel like moving into love, move into love – don't choose! And when you feel like moving into meditation, move into meditation – don't choose! There is no need to choose.

And the desire for both never arises together. That is something tremendously significant to be understood: the desire for both never arises together. It is impossible – because love means the desire to be with somebody else; love means to be focused on the other. And meditation means to forget the other and be focused on oneself. Both desires cannot arise together.

When you want to be with somebody else, that means you are tired of yourself. And when you want to be with yourself, that means you are tired of the other. It is a beautiful rhythm! Being with the other creates a deep desire in you to be alone. You can ask lovers – all lovers feel that desire to be alone arising sometimes. But they are afraid to be alone because they think it is going against love, and what will the partner say? The other person may feel offended. So they pretend –

even though they want to be alone, they want their own space, they pretend and they go on being together. That pretence is false, it is destructive of love. And it makes your relationship phoney.

When you feel like being alone, with all respect, with all love, tell the other, 'A great desire to be alone is arising in me, and I have to go into it – there is no question of choice. Please don't feel offended. It is nothing to do with you; it is simply my own inner rhythm.'

And this will also help the other person to be authentic and true with you. And, slowly, if you really love a person, the rhythms start falling into a togetherness, and that is the miracle, the magic of love. If there is genuine love between two persons, this outcome is inevitable. The two people will start to find that the desire to be together and the desire to be separate arise at the same times. They will become a rhythm: sometimes coming together and being together and dissolved into each other, forgetting all about themselves; and then sometimes arising out of each other, moving, withdrawing, separating, into their own spaces, becoming their own selves – becoming meditators.

Between meditation and love, there is no choice. Both have to be lived in their own rhythm. And whatever is arising in you, whatever is the deeper longing of the moment, move with the longing.

accept the ups and downs

One has to become more accepting of all the ups and downs in life. There is a rhythm: sometimes you will feel that you are in tune, sometimes you will feel that you are not in tune; that is natural. It is like day and night, summer and winter. One has to learn the shadow part of everything. If you cannot accept the shadow part, you become unnecessarily disturbed, and that disturbance will make things more complicated.

When something beautiful happens, accept it, feel grateful; when it doesn't happen, accept that too and continue to feel grateful, knowing that this is just a resting period. For the whole day you have worked, and at night you fall asleep – don't feel miserable because you are not able to work and earn money and do a thousand and one things at the same time, and because there are so many things to do. Don't worry about it!

There are people who do worry. Then they start losing sleep, which does not benefit them. The person who has not been able to sleep in the night feels exhausted in the morning. The person who forgets the whole day and accepts night as a rest, and goes into deep relaxation, will be able to live again in the morning with new eyes and new being.

Always remember that everything has its rest period. And the rest period is not against the activity; the rest period gives it energy, vitality, new life.

don't fight with your nature

the psychologist Hans Selye worked throughout his whole life on only one problem – stress. And he came to certain very profound conclusions. One is that stress is not always wrong; it can be used in beautiful ways. It is not necessarily negative – and if we think that it is always negative, that it is not good, then we create problems. Stress in itself can be used as a stepping stone, it can become a creative force. But we have generally been taught that stress is bad, so that when you are under any kind of stress you become afraid. And your fear makes it even more stressful; the situation is not helped by it.

For example, perhaps economic problems are creating stress. The moment you feel that there is some tension, some stress, you become afraid of it. You tell yourself, 'I have to relax.' Now, trying to relax will not help, because you cannot relax; in fact, trying to relax will create a new kind of stress. The stress is there and you are trying to relax and you cannot, so you are compounding the problem.

When stress is there, use it as creative energy. First, accept it; there is no need to fight with it. Accept it, it is perfectly okay. It simply says, 'There are economic problems, something is going wrong, you may lose out.' Stress is simply an indication that the body is getting ready to take on the situation. If you try to relax or you take painkillers or tranquillizers, you are going against the body.

The body is getting ready to deal with a certain situation, a certain challenge that is there. Enjoy the challenge! Even if you sometimes can't sleep at night, there is no need to be worried. Use the energy that arises from stress: walk up and down, go for a run, go for a long walk. Plan what you want to do, what the mind wants to do. Rather than trying to go to sleep, which is not possible, use the situation in a creative way. The mind is simply saying that the body is ready to contend with a problem; this is no time to relax. Relaxation can take place later on.

In fact, if you have lived through your stress totally, you will come to relaxation automatically; you can only go on so far, then the body automatically relaxes. If you want to relax in the middle you create trouble; the body cannot relax in the middle. It is almost as if an Olympic runner is getting ready, just waiting for the starting gun, the signal, and he will be off, he will go like the wind. He is full of stress; this is no time to relax. If he takes a tranquillizer he will be of no use in the race. Or if he relaxes and tries to do Transcendental Meditation he will lose completely. He has to use his stress: the stress is boiling, it is gathering energy. He is becoming more and more vital and full of potential. Now he has to sit on this stress and use it as energy, as fuel.

Selye has given a new name to this kind of stress: he calls it 'eustress' – like euphoria. It is a positive stress. After the runner has finished running he will fall into deep sleep; the problem is solved. Now there is no problem, the stress disappears of its own accord.

So try this too: when there is a stressful situation don't freak out, don't become afraid of it. Go into it, use it to fight with. A human being has tremendous energy, and the more you use it, the more you will have of it.

When there is a stressful situation, fight – do all that you can do, go madly into it. Allow it, accept it and welcome it. Stress is good, it prepares you to fight. And when you have worked it out, you will be surprised: great relaxation comes, and that relaxation is not created by you. Maybe for two or three days you cannot sleep and then for 48 hours you can't wake up, and that is okay!

We go on carrying many wrong notions – for example, that every person has to sleep eight hours every day. It depends what the situation is. There are situations when no sleep is needed: your house is on fire, and you are trying to sleep. Now that is not possible and that should not be possible, otherwise who is going to put that fire out? And when the house is on fire, all other things are put aside; suddenly your body is ready to fight the fire. You will not feel sleepy. When the fire has gone out and everything has settled down, you may fall asleep for a long period, and that will do.

People don't all need the same amount of sleep either. A few people can manage with two hours, three hours, four hours, five hours; others need six, eight, ten, twelve.

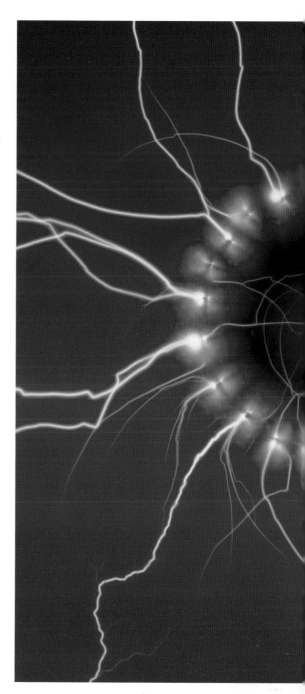

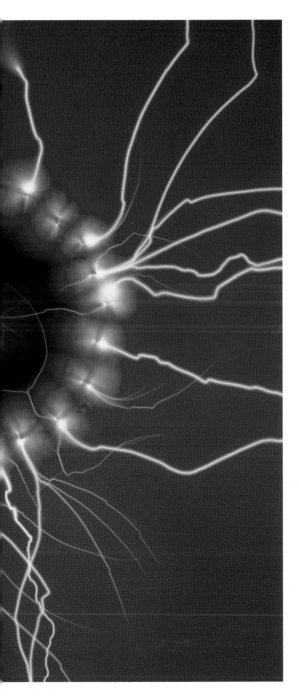

People differ, there is no norm. And people experience stress differently too.

There are two kinds of people in the world: one can be called the racehorse type and the other is the turtle type. If the racehorse type is not allowed to go fast, to go at things with speed, he will suffer from stress; he has to go at his pace. So if you are a racehorse, forget about relaxation and things like that; they are not for you. They are for turtles! Just be a racehorse if that is natural to you, and don't think of the joys that turtles are enjoying; that is not for you. You have a different kind of joy. If a turtle starts becoming a racehorse he will be in the same trouble!

So accept your nature. If you are a fighter, a warrior, you have to be that way and that's your joy. There is no need to be afraid, go into it wholeheartedly. Compete in the marketplace, do all that you really want to do. Don't be afraid of the consequences and accept the stress. One has to understand one's type. Once the type is understood there is no problem; then one can follow a clear-cut line.

look for the pay-off

If you find that you go on creating unhappiness for yourself, you must be getting something out of it; otherwise, why would you create unhappiness? Sometimes misery can give you tremendous benefits. You may not be aware of the benefits, you may be unconscious of them, so you go on thinking, 'Why do I go on creating misery?' And you are not aware that your misery is giving you something that you want.

For example, whenever you are miserable, people are sympathetic towards you. If you are miserable, your husband comes and puts his hand on your head, massages you, is very loving, pays attention to you. When you are in misery there are many benefits.

Just look around. In the morning, children immediately start feeling stomach-aches the moment the bus arrives and they have to go to school. And you know it! You know why Johnny has a stomach-ache. But it is the same case with you. It may be a little more sophisticated, more cunning, more rationalized, but it is the same.

When people start failing in their lives, they create high blood pressure, heart attacks and all kinds of problems. They are rationalizations. Have you ever noticed? Heart attacks and high blood pressure often occur around the age of 42. Why near the age of 42? Suddenly a healthy person becomes a victim of a heart attack.

At the age of 42, life comes to a certain conclusion – whether you have failed or succeeded. Because beyond 42 there is not much hope: if you have made money, you have made it by now – because the greatest days of energy and power have passed. The peak age is 35. You can give seven more years; in fact, you have been going downhill for seven years already. But you have done everything that you could do. And now the age has come, 42, and suddenly you see that you have failed.

Now you need some rationalization ... immediately a heart attack comes. That's a great boon, a blessing from God. Now you can fall into bed and you can say, 'What can I do? The heart attack disturbed everything. Just when everything was going okay, when I was about to succeed, make a name for myself or make money, this heart attack came.' Now the heart attack is a beautiful camouflage; now nobody can say that you are at fault, that you didn't work hard, that you are not intelligent enough. Nobody can say anything like that to you. Now people will feel sympathy for you; they will all be kind to you and they will say, 'What can you do? It is fate.'

Misery is chosen again and again because it gives something to you, and you have to see what it is giving to you – only then can you drop it. You need to look deeply into what your misery gives you; otherwise you

If prisons were beautiful places, then who would want to leave them?

cannot drop it. Unless you are ready to drop the benefits, you cannot drop the misery.

If prisons were beautiful places, then who would want to leave them? And if you are not trying to get out of your prison, look again ... there must be something keeping you there – wall-to-wall carpets, colour television, air-conditioning, beautiful paintings. There are no bars on the windows, there is nobody guarding you – you have an absolute sense of freedom! So why should you try to escape from it? The question is not how to get out of it; the question is how to stay in it!

Look again at your misery; don't condemn it from the very beginning. If you condemn it from the very beginning, you will not be able to watch, you will not be able to observe. In fact, don't even call it misery, because our words have connotations. When you call it misery, you have already condemned it; and when you condemn something, you are closed to it, you don't look at it. Call it XYZ – it makes little difference. Call it X, whatever the situation is, be a little mathematical – call it X, and then go into it and see what it is, what its benefits are, what the main reasons are that you go on creating it, why you cling to it. And you will be surprised: what you have been calling misery contains many things that you enjoy. And unless you have seen this,

and looked into those things that you enjoy about it, you will not be able to change anything. Then there are two possibilities.

One possibility is that you stop thinking of getting out of this pattern – that is one possibility, because the benefits are so great that you accept it. And accepting the pattern is a transformation. The second possibility is that you see that your unhappiness is created by you yourself, by your own unconscious desires, and that those unconscious desires are stupid. Seeing the whole stupidity of it, you no longer support it. It disappears of its own accord. These are the two possibilities: your support disappears and the misery is evaporated, or you simply accept it because you like all the things that it brings to you, you welcome it – and in that very welcome, again the misery disappears!

These are the two sides of the same coin. But understanding is needed, total understanding of your misery – and then you can be transformed. Either you will drop everything out of that understanding or you will accept everything. These are the two ways, the negative and the positive, for the transformation to happen.

look for the changing, appreciate the unchanging

i n a way, every day is the same. How can it be otherwise? The same sun, the same sun rising every morning, and the same sunset, yes – but if you watch closely, have you ever seen two sunrises exactly the same? Have you ever watched the colours in the sky? Have you ever seen the cloud formations around the sun?

No two sunrises are the same; no two sunsets are the same. The world is a discontinuous continuity – discontinuous because every moment something new is happening and yet continuous because it is not absolutely new. It is connected. So it is true that there is nothing new under the sun, and at the same time there is nothing old under the sun. Both are true.

Nothing is new and nothing is old. Everything goes on changing yet somehow remains the same, somehow remains the same and yet goes on changing. That's the beauty, the mystery, the secret. You cannot reduce it to any formula: you cannot say it is the same, you cannot say it is not the same. You cannot reduce life into your categories; your pigeonholes are just worthless. When it comes to life, you have to drop all your pigeonholes, your categories. It is bigger than your categories, transcendental to all categories. It is so vast that you cannot find its beginning or its end.

Yesterday I was here, but I am not the same. How can I be? In that time, so much

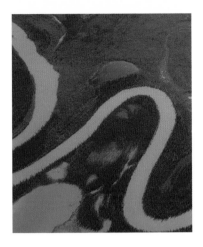 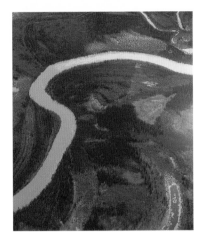 

Everything goes on changing yet somehow remains the same...

water has flowed down the Ganges. I am 24 hours older, 24 hours of experience have been added to me, 24 hours of awareness. I am richer; I'm not the same – death has come a little closer. You are also not the same, and yet I look the same and you look the same.

You can see the point. This is what I mean when I say life is a mystery: you cannot classify it, you cannot say definitely that it is so. The moment you say it, immediately you will become aware that life has contradicted you.

Are the trees the same as they were yesterday? Many leaves have fallen, many new leaves have grown. Many flowers are gone, many flowers have risen higher. How can they be the same? See, today the birds are not singing. It is so silent. Yesterday the birds were singing. It was a different silence, it was full of song. Today's silence is different; it is not full of song. Even the wind is not blowing – everything has stopped. Yesterday there was a strong wind. The trees are meditating today; yesterday they were dancing. It cannot be the same, and yet, it is the same.

It depends on you – how you look at life. If you look at it as if it is the same, you will be bored. Don't throw your responsibility on to somebody else. It is your outlook. If you say it is the same, then you will be bored.

If you see the constant change, flux-like, the great whirlwind-like movement all around you, the dynamism of life, each moment the old disappearing and the new coming in – if you can see the continuous birth – then you will be enchanted, thrilled. Your life will not be boring. You will be continuously wondering, 'What next?' You will not be dull. Your intelligence will remain sharp, alive and young.

Now it depends on what you want. If you want to become like a dead person, stupid, dull, gloomy, sad and bored, then believe that life is the same. If you want to become young and alive, fresh, radiant, then believe that life is new each moment.

Says the Greek philosopher Heraclitus, 'You cannot step twice into the same river.'

You cannot meet the same person twice and you cannot see the same sunrise twice. It is up to you. And if you understand me, I will say, don't choose. If you choose the idea that everything is old, you become old. If you choose that everything is young and new, you become young. If you understand me, I say don't choose; see that both are true. Then you transcend all categories. You are neither old nor young. Then you become eternal, then you become godlike, then you become like life itself.

Something new, constantly happening, makes you alive...

If you believe that everything is the same, then you are going to be bored. The repetition will kill you. To be sharp and alive, one needs something that is not repetitive. Something new, constantly happening, makes you alive, keeps you alive, keeps you alert.

Have you ever watched a dog sitting silently? A rock is lying just in front of him; he will not be worried. But let the rock start moving. Just have a small thread connected to the rock and pull it, and the dog will jump. He will start barking. Movement makes him sharp; then all dullness is gone. Then he is no longer sleepy. He is no longer daydreaming. He will simply jump out of his slumber. Something has changed.

Change gives you movement, but constant change can also be very unsettling. As constant sameness can be deadening, constant change can uproot you.

That is happening in the West; people are always changing their lives. The statisticians say that in the USA the average limit of a person doing a job is three years. People are changing their jobs, changing their towns, changing their spouses, trying to change everything – changing their car every year, their house – their values have changed. In England they make the Rolls Royce. The idea is that it lasts for ever, a lifetime at least. In America they make beautiful cars, but durability is not a quality to be bothered about because who is going to keep a car for his whole life? If it lasts for one year, that's enough. When the American goes to purchase a car, he does not bother about durability; he asks about exchangeability. Americans live in a world of change – everything is changing – but then Americans have lost their roots.

I was always surprised going back to my village in India. The first thing that I would see was that there, time stands still. Everything seems to be eternally the same. But then the people have roots. They are dull, but they are very rooted. They are very comfortable, happy. They are not alienated. They don't feel like strangers. How can they feel like strangers when everything is so familiar? When they were born it was the same; when they die it will be the same. Everything is so stable. How can you feel like a stranger? The whole town is like a small family.

In America, everything is uprooted. Nobody knows where they belong. The very sense of belonging is lost. If you ask somebody 'Where do you belong?' he will shrug his shoulders — because he has been to so many towns, to so many colleges, to so many universities. He cannot even be certain of who he is because identity is very loose, fluid. In a way it is good because the person remains sharp and alive, but the roots have gone.

Both things have been tried: stability, rootedness, nothing new under the sun – we tried it in the past, for many centuries.

It rusted the human mind. People were comfortable but not very alive. Then in America, something new happened and it is spreading all over the world, because America is the future of the world. Whatever is happening there is going to happen everywhere, sooner or later. America sets the trend. Now people are very alive but unrooted and don't know where they belong. A great desire to belong has arisen. A great desire to be rooted somewhere, to possess someone and to be possessed by someone: something durable, something stable, something like a centre – because people are moving like wheels and there seems to be no rest. And it is very stressful, continuously changing, continuously changing. And change is accelerating every day, becoming faster and faster. Everything is in such great flux and turmoil and chaos, and people feel deeply stressed, under great strain and tension.

Both have their benefits and both have their curses. A synthesis has to be made between these two orientations. One should be aware that life is both the old and the new together, simultaneously – old because the whole past is present in the present moment; new because the whole future is potentially present in the present moment. The present moment is a culmination of the whole past and the beginning of the whole future. In this moment, all that has happened is hidden, and all that is going to happen is also hidden. Each moment is past and future both, a convergence of past and future. So something is old and something is new, and if you can become aware of both

together, you will have sharpness and roots both together. You will be at ease, without any stress. You will not become dull, and you will be very conscious and alert.

I heard this story.

Mrs MacMahon went berserk one afternoon. She broke every dish and cup and reduced her usually spotless kitchen to a shambles. The police arrived and took her to the city's mental institution. The head psychiatrist sent for her husband.

'Do you know any reason,' asked the doctor, 'why your wife should suddenly lose her mind?'

'I'm just as surprised as you are,' answered Mr MacMahon. 'I can't imagine what got into her. She has always been such a quiet, hardworking woman. Why, she has not been out of the kitchen in twenty years!'

It is clear why Mrs MacMahon went mad. It is as simple as 'two plus two make four'. If for twenty years one has not been out of the kitchen, it is maddening. But the opposite is also maddening. If you haven't been to your home for twenty years, and have become just a traveller, always moving and never arriving anywhere, always reaching and never reaching anywhere; if you have become a gypsy and you don't have any home, then you too will start going mad.

Both situations are dangerous taken separately. Taken together they make life very rich. All polarities make life rich: yin and yang, man and woman, dark and light, life and death, god and devil, saint and sinner. Without polarities, life becomes monotonous. Don't choose a monotonous life. Become richer.

part three

relating from the centre

All relationships are mirror-like. You see your
face in the mirror of the other's being. It is
very difficult to see your own face directly –
you will need the other, the mirror, to see
your own face. And where can you find a
better mirror than the eyes of the other?

Look sometimes into the eyes of your
enemy and you will see a facet of your being.
Look sometimes into the eyes of your lover,
your friend, and you will see another facet of
your being. Look into the eyes of a person
who is indifferent to you and you will see yet
another facet of your being. Collect all these
facets – they are yours, different aspects of
your being. In different situations, with
different people, in different worlds, move ...
and gather all this richness and awareness
and alertness and consciousness. Then go
back to the centre and take all this awareness
with you, and your meditation will be deeper
and richer.

living with others: the rules and when to break them

everybody is born in freedom, but dies in bondage. The beginning of life is totally loose and natural, but then enters the society, then enter rules and regulations, morality, discipline and many sorts of training, and the looseness and the naturalness and the spontaneous being are lost. One starts to gather around oneself a sort of armour. One starts becoming more and more rigid. The inner softness is no longer apparent.

On the boundary of one's being, one creates a fort-like phenomenon, to defend, to not be vulnerable, to react, to create security and safety. The freedom of being is lost. One starts looking at others' eyes.

Their approval, their denial, their condemnation or appreciation becomes more and more valuable. The others become the criterion, and one starts to imitate and follow others.

One has to live with others – and a child is very soft, he can be moulded in any way; society starts moulding him – the parents, the teachers, the school – and by and by he becomes a character rather than a being. He learns all the rules. He either becomes a conformist or he becomes rebellious; both are a sort of bondage. If he becomes a conformist, orthodox, 'square', that is one sort of bondage. Alternatively, he can react, become a hippie, and move to the other extreme, but that too is a sort of bondage because reaction depends on the same thing it reacts against. You may go to the opposite corner, but deep down in the mind you are rebelling against the same rules. Others are following them, you are reacting to them, but the focus remains on the same rules. Reactionaries or revolutionaries, all travel in the same boat. They may be standing against each other, back to back, but the boat is the same.

A centred person is neither a reactionary nor a revolutionary. A centred person is loose and natural; he is neither for something nor against, he is simply himself. He has no rules to follow and no rules to refuse. He simply has no rules. A centred person is free in his

A centred person is loose and natural ... he is simply himself.

own being, he is not moulded by habits and conditioning. He is not a 'cultured' being – not that he is uncivilized and primitive, he is the highest flowering of civilization and culture, but he is not a cultured being. He has grown in his awareness and he doesn't need any rules, he has transcended rules. He is truthful not because there is a rule to be truthful. But in being loose and natural he is simply truthful; it simply happens that he is truthful. He has compassion, not because he follows a precept to be compassionate, no. Being loose and natural, he simply feels compassion flowing all around. That is nothing deliberate, it is just a by-product of his growth in awareness. He is not against society, nor for society – he is simply beyond it. He has again become a child, a child of an absolutely unknown world, a child in a new dimension – he is reborn.

Every child is born natural and loose; then society comes in – it has to come in for certain reasons. Nothing is wrong with this, because if the child is left to himself or herself the child will never grow, and the child will become just like an animal. Society has to come in; society has to be passed through – it is needed. The only thing to remember is that it is just a passage to pass through. One should not make one's house in it. Society has to be followed and then transcended; the rules have to be learned and then unlearned.

The rules will come into your life because there are others. You are not alone. The child in the mother's womb is absolutely alone, no rules are needed, no morality, no discipline, no order. Rules come only when the 'other' comes into one's life; the rules come with relationships – because you are not alone, you have to think of others and consider them. The moment the child is born, even the first breath he takes is social. If the child does not cry, the doctors will force him to cry immediately, because if he doesn't cry for a few minutes then he will be dead. He has to cry because the crying opens the passage through which he will be able to breathe, it clears the throat. He has to be forced to cry because others are there and the moulding has started.

Nothing is wrong with this. It has to be done, but in such a way that the child never loses his awareness, does not become identified with the cultured pattern, remains free deep inside, knows that rules have to be followed but that rules are not life, and knows also that he has to be taught. And this is what a good society will teach: 'These rules are good because you have to live with others, but these rules are not absolute. You are not expected to remain confined by them – one day you must transcend them.' A society is good if it teaches its members both civilization and transcendence.

You have to listen to others to a certain extent, and then you have to start listening to yourself. You must come back to the original state in the end. Before you die, you must

become an innocent child again – loose and natural, because in death you enter once more the dimension of being alone. Just as you were in the womb, in death again you will enter into the realm of being alone. No society exists there. And in the whole of your life you have to find a few spaces in your life, a few moments like oases in the desert, when you simply close your eyes and go beyond society, move into yourself, into your own womb – this is what meditation is. Society is there; you simply close your eyes and forget society and become alone. No rules exist here, no character is needed, no morality, no words, no language. You can be loose and natural inside.

Grow into that loose-and-naturalness. Even if there is a need for outer discipline, inside you can remain wild. If one can remain wild inside and still practise the things that are needed in society, then soon one can come to a point where one simply transcends.

...everybody is prodding you ... to go in yet another direction...

I will tell you a story; it is a Sufi story.

An old man and a young man are travelling with a donkey. They have come near a town and they are walking with their donkey.

Schoolchildren pass them. They giggle and laugh and say, 'Look at these fools: they have a healthy donkey with them and they are walking. At least the old man could sit on the donkey.'

Listening to these children, the old man and the young man ask themselves, 'What should we do? People are laughing and soon we will be entering the town, so it is better to follow what they are saying.' So the old man sits on the donkey and the young man follows.

Then they come near another group of people who look at them and say, 'Look! The old man is sitting on the donkey and the poor boy is walking. This is absurd! The old man can walk, but the boy should be allowed to sit on the donkey.' So they change places; the old man starts walking and the boy sits on the donkey.

Then another group comes and says, 'Look at these fools. This boy seems very arrogant. Maybe the old man is his father or his teacher but the old man is walking, and the young man is sitting on the donkey – this is against all the rules!'

So what should they do now? They decide that there is only one possibility – they should both sit on the donkey. So they both sit on the donkey. Then some more people come and they say, 'Look at these people, so violent! The poor donkey is almost dying. Two people on one donkey? It would be better to carry the donkey on their shoulders.'

So the two men have another discussion, and then see that they are approaching the river and the bridge. They have now almost reached the boundary of the town, so they decide, 'It is better to do as people in this town say, otherwise they will think we are fools.' So they find a piece of bamboo; on their shoulders they tie the donkey's legs together, tie him to the piece of bamboo and carry him between them. The donkey tries to rebel, as donkeys do (they cannot be forced very easily). He tries to escape because he is not a believer in society and what others say. But the two men are too strong, so the donkey has to yield.

Just in the middle of the bridge a crowd is passing, and they all gather, saying, 'Look, what fools! We have never seen such idiots – a donkey is to ride upon, not to carry on your shoulders. Have you gone mad?'

Listening to them – it is a huge crowd – the donkey becomes restless, so restless that he jumps free and falls from the bridge down into the river. Both men go down to the river. The donkey is dead. They sit down on the river bank and the old man says, 'Now listen ... '

This is not an ordinary story – the old man was a Sufi master, an enlightened person, and the young man was a disciple. The old master was trying to give him a lesson, because Sufis always create situations; they say that unless the real situation exists, you cannot learn from it properly. So this was just a scenario for the young man. Now the old man said, 'Look – just like this donkey, you will be dead if you listen to people too much. Don't bother about what others say, because there are millions of others and they have their own minds and everybody will say something different; everybody has his or her opinions and if you listen to opinions it will be the end of you.'

Don't listen to anybody, but remain yourself. Just bypass others, be indifferent. If you go on listening to everybody, they will all be prodding you this way or that. You will never be able to reach your innermost centre.

Everybody has become eccentric. This English word is very beautiful: it means off the centre, and we use it to describe mad people. But everybody is eccentric, off centre. And the whole world is helping you to become eccentric because everybody is prodding you. Your mother is prodding you towards north, your father towards south; your uncle is telling you one thing, your brother something else. Your wife, of course, is prodding you to go in yet another direction – everybody is trying to force you somewhere. By and by, a moment comes when you are nowhere. You remain just on the crossroads being pushed from north to south, from south to east, from east to west, moving nowhere. By and by, this becomes your whole life – you become eccentric. This is the situation. And if you go on listening to others and not listening to your inner centre, this situation will continue.

The purpose of all meditation is to become centred, not to be eccentric – to come to your own centre.

Listen to your inner voice, feel it, and move with that feeling. By and by, you will be able to laugh at others' opinions, or you can simply be indifferent. And once you become centred you become a powerful being; then nobody can prod you, nobody can push you anywhere – simply, nobody dares. You are such a power, centred in yourself, that anybody who comes with an opinion about you simply forgets her opinion when she is near you. Anybody who comes to push you somewhere simply forgets that he had come to push. Rather, just coming near you he starts feeling overpowered by you.

That's how even a single person can become so powerful that the whole society, the whole of history, cannot push him a single inch. That's how a Buddha exists, a Jesus. You can kill a Jesus but you cannot push him. You can destroy his body, but you cannot push him a single inch. Not that he is adamant or stubborn, no, it is simply that he is centred in his own being. He knows what is good for him, and he knows what is blissful for him. It has already happened; now you cannot lure him towards new goals; no salesmanship can lure him to any other goal. He has found his home. He can listen to you patiently, but you cannot move him. He is centred.

This centring is the first step towards becoming natural and loose; without centring, if you are natural and loose, anybody can take you anywhere. That's why children are not allowed to be natural and loose; they are not mature enough to be like that. If they are natural and loose and running all around, their life will be wasted. Hence I say society does a necessary job: it protects them, enclosing them like a citadel. Children need it; they are very vulnerable, they can be destroyed by anybody. The multitude is there, they will not be able to find their way – they need character armour.

But if that character armour becomes your total life, then you are lost. You should not become the citadel; you should remain the master and you should remain capable of going out of it. Otherwise it is not a protection, it becomes a prison. You should be capable of going out of your character. You should be capable of putting aside your principles. You should be capable, if the situation demands, of responding in an absolutely novel way. If this capacity is lost then you become rigid, and you cannot be loose. If this capacity is lost then you become unnatural, and you are not flexible.

Flexibility is youth, rigidity is old age; the more flexible, the younger; the more rigid, the older. Death is absolute rigidity. Life is absolute looseness, flexibility.

This you have to remember.

start from the centre

life on the outside is a cyclone – a constant conflict, turmoil, struggle. But it is only so on the surface – just as on the surface of the ocean are waves, maddening noise, constant struggle. But this is not all of life. Deep down there is also a centre – soundless, silent, with no conflict, no struggle. At the centre, life is a noiseless flow, relaxed, a river moving with no struggle, with no fight, no violence. You can become identified with the surface, with the outer. Then anxiety and anguish follow. This is what has happened to everyone; we are identified with the surface and with the struggle that goes on there.

The surface is bound to be disturbed, there is nothing wrong with that. But if you can be rooted at the centre, the disturbance on the surface will become beautiful; it will have a beauty of its own. If you can be silent within, then all the sounds without become musical. Then nothing is wrong; it becomes a play. But if you don't know the inner core, the silent centre, if you are totally identified with the surface, you will go mad. And almost everyone is mad.

Various techniques, such as yoga, meditation, Zen, basically help you to restore contact with the centre. They are ways to help you to move within, to forget the periphery, to leave the periphery for a time and relax into your own being so deeply that the outer disappears and only the inner remains. Once you know how to move inwards, how to step down into yourself, it is not difficult. But if you don't know, if all you know is the mind clinging to the surface, it is very difficult. Relaxing into one's self is not difficult: not clinging to the surface is.

I once heard this Sufi story.

Once it happened that a Sufi fakir was travelling. It was a dark night and he lost his way. It was so dark that he couldn't even see where he was going – then suddenly he took a step and there was no ground beneath his feet. He caught hold of a branch and saved himself from falling, but he was terrified. He didn't know what was down there in the darkness or how deep the abyss was. The night was cold. He cried out for help but there was no one to listen, only his own voice echoed back. The night was so cold that his hands were becoming frozen and he knew that sooner or later he would have to let go of the branch – it was going to be difficult to keep holding on. He was already losing his grip. Death was absolutely near; any moment he would fall and die. And then the last moment came. You can understand how terrified he was. Dying moment by moment, then the last moment came and he felt the branch slipping out of his hands. There was no way to hold on, so he had to fall. But the moment he fell...

He started dancing! There was no abyss, he was on firm ground! And he had suffered all night...

This is our situation. We go on clinging to the surface, afraid that if we leave the surface we will be lost. Actually, in clinging to the surface we are lost. But deep down there is darkness and we cannot see any ground; we cannot see anything else but the surface.

All meditation techniques are to make you courageous, strong, adventurous, so that you can stop holding on to the surface and fall within yourself. That which looks like an abyss, dark, bottomless, is the very ground of your being. Once you leave the surface, the periphery, you will be centred.

This centring is the aim of meditation. Once you are centred you can move to the periphery but you will be totally different.

The quality of your consciousness will have changed altogether. Then you can move to the periphery but you will never be the periphery again – you will remain at the centre. And remaining centred while you are engaged in activities at the periphery is beautiful. Then you can enjoy it; it will become a beautiful play. Then there is no conflict; it is all a game. Then what happens on the periphery will not create tensions within you and there will be no anguish and no anxiety around you.

And any moment that it becomes too much, too heavy on you, you can go back to the original source – you can have a dip in the centre of your being. Then you will be refreshed, rejuvenated, and you can move to the periphery again.

Once you know the way, you can do this – and the way is not long. You are not going anywhere else than into your own self so it is not a long way; it is just nearby. The only barrier is your holding on, clinging to the periphery, afraid that if you leave it you will be lost.

The fear feels just as if you are going to die. Moving to the inner centre is a death, in a way – death in the sense that your identity with the periphery will die and a new sense of your own being will arise.

drop the doing

If we want to say in a few words what meditation techniques are, we can say that they are a deep relaxation into oneself, a total relaxation into oneself.

We are always tense; that is our holding, our clinging. We are never relaxed, never in a state of let-go. We are always doing something – that doing is the problem. We are never in a state of non-doing, when things are happening and one is just there, not doing anything. Breath comes in and goes out, the blood circulates, the body is alive and throbbing, the breeze blows, the world goes on spinning around – and you are not doing anything; you are not a doer. You are simply relaxed and things are happening.

When things are happening and you are not a doer, you are totally relaxed. When you are a doer and things are not happening but are being manipulated by you, you are tense.

You relax partially while you are asleep, but it is not total. Even in your sleep you go on manipulating, even in your sleep you don't allow everything to happen. Watch a person sleeping – you will see that his whole body is very tense. Watch a small child sleeping; he is very relaxed. Or watch an animal, a cat – a cat is always relaxed. You are not relaxed even while asleep; you are tense, struggling, moving, fighting with something. On your face there are tensions. In dreams you may be fighting, protecting something or someone, doing the same things

If you know how to relax then nothing can disturb you.

as when you are awake, repeating them in an inner drama. You are not relaxed; you are not in a deep let-go.

That's why sleep is becoming more and more difficult for people. And psychologists say that if the same trend continues, soon the day will come when no one will be able to sleep naturally. Sleep will have to be chemically induced because no one will be able to fall asleep naturally. The day is not very far off. People are already on the way towards it because even while asleep they are only partially asleep, partially relaxed.

Meditation is the deepest sleep. It is total relaxation plus something more; one is totally relaxed and yet alert. Awareness is there. Total sleep with awareness is meditation. Fully alert, things are happening but you are not resisting, not fighting, not doing. The doer is not there; the doer has gone into sleep. Only a witness is there; a non-doing alertness is there. Then nothing can disturb you.

If you know how to relax then nothing can disturb you. If you don't know how to relax then everything will disturb you – and I say everything. It is not really something in particular that disturbs you, everything is just an excuse. You are almost always ready to be disturbed. If one thing doesn't disturb you, then something else will; you will get disturbed. You are ready, you have a tendency to get disturbed. If all the causes are

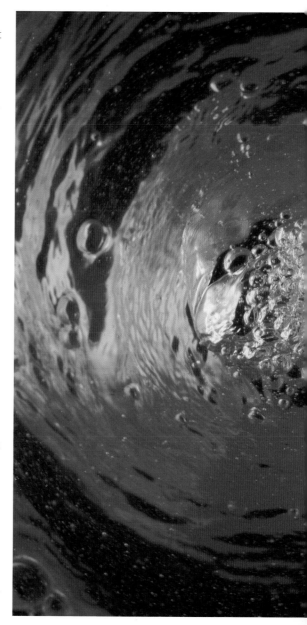

If you don't know how to relax then everything will disturb you.

withdrawn from you, even then you will get disturbed. You will create some cause. If nothing comes from without, you will create something from within – some thought, some idea – and you will get disturbed. But you need excuses.

Once you know how to relax, nothing can disturb you. Not that the world will change, not that things will be different – the world will be the same. But you won't have the tendency, you won't have the madness; you will not be constantly ready to be disturbed. Then all that happens around you is soothing – even the traffic noise becomes soothing if you are relaxed. Even the marketplace becomes soothing. It depends on you. It is an inner quality.

The more you go towards the centre, the more the quality of relaxation arises, and the more you move towards the periphery the more you will be disturbed. If you are prone to be disturbed, that shows only one thing: that you are existing near the periphery – nothing else. It is an indication that you have made your abode near the surface. And this is a false abode because your real home is at the centre, the very centre of your being.

the peaceful heart

the ancient treatise known as the Vigyan Bhairav Tantra of Shiva gives this technique: In any easy position gradually pervade an area between the armpits into great peace.

This is a very simple method but it works miraculously – try it. Anyone can try it; there is no danger involved. The first thing is to be in an easy, relaxed position – relaxed in a position that is easy for you. Don't try to force yourself into a particular position. Buddha sits in a particular posture; it is easy for him. It can also become easy for you if you practise it for a time, but at the very beginning it will not be easy for you. And there is no need to practise it: start from any posture that comes easily to you right now. Don't struggle with the posture. You can sit in an easy chair and relax. The main thing is that your body should be in a relaxed state.

So just close your eyes and feel ... all over the body. Start with the legs – feel whether there is some tension there or not. If you feel there is some tension, make it more tense. If you feel there is some tension in the right leg, then make that tension as intense as possible. Bring it to a peak – then suddenly relax so that you can feel how the relaxation settles there. Then go all over the body just looking everywhere for tension. Wherever you feel the tension, make it more so, because it is easy to relax when it is intense. Otherwise it is very difficult because you cannot really feel it. It is easy to move from one extreme to another, very easy, because the extreme itself creates the situation to move to the opposite. If you feel some tension in the face, then strain all the facial muscles as much as possible, create tension and bring it to a peak. Bring it to a point where you feel that no more is possible – then suddenly relax. In this way, see that all the limbs and all parts of the body are relaxed.

Be particular about the facial muscles, because they carry 90 per cent of your tensions – the rest of the body carries only 10 per cent. Most of your tensions are in the mind, so the face becomes the storage place for these tensions. So screw up your face as much as possible, don't be shy about it. Make it intensely anguished, anxious – and then suddenly relax.

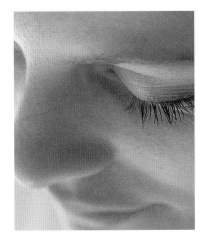
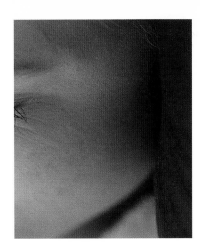

Just feel that the body is relaxed and then forget the body.

Do this exploration of tensions in the body for five minutes so that you can feel that every part of the whole body is relaxed. Now this is an easy posture for you. You can do it sitting, or lying in bed or however you feel is easy for you.

In any easy position gradually pervade an area between the armpits into great peace.

The second thing: when you feel that the body has come to an easy posture, don't pay too much attention to it. Just feel that the body is relaxed and then forget the body. Because really, remembering the body is a sort of tension. That's why I say not to pay attention to it. Relax the body and forget about it. Forgetting is relaxation. Whenever you remember too much, that very remembering brings a tension to the body.

You may not have observed this, but there is a very easy experiment you can try. First take your pulse. Then close your eyes, bring your attention to your pulse for five minutes, and then take it again. The pulse will now be beating faster because the attention brings tension to it. When a doctor takes your pulse, it is never accurate – it is always faster than it was before the doctor started taking it. When the doctor takes your hand in his hand, you become alert.

Whenever you bring your consciousness to any part of the body, that part becomes tense. You become tense when someone else observes you; the whole body becomes tense. When you are alone you are different. When someone enters the room you are not the same; the whole body starts functioning at a faster rate. You have become tense. So don't make much fuss about relaxation or you will become obsessed with it. For five minutes simply relax easily and then forget about it. Your forgetting will be helpful and it will bring a deeper relaxation to the body.

Gradually pervade an area between the armpits into great peace.

Close your eyes and just feel the area between the two armpits: the heart area, your chest. First feel it just between the two armpits with your total attention, total awareness. Forget the rest of the body, take notice just of the heart area between the two armpits, the chest, and feel it filled with great peace.

The moment the body is relaxed, peace automatically happens in your heart. The heart becomes silent, relaxed, harmonious. And when you forget the rest of the body and bring your attention just to the chest and consciously feel it filled with peace, great peace will come immediately.

If you can find peace directly ... your whole life will be filled with love.

There are areas in the body, specific centres, where particular feelings can be created consciously. Between the two armpits is the heart centre, and the heart centre is the source of all the peace that happens to you, whenever it happens. Whenever you are peaceful, the peace is coming from the heart. The heart radiates peace. That is why people all over the world, every people, without any distinction of religion, country or culture, have felt that love arises from somewhere near the heart. No scientific explanation exists. Whenever you think of love you think of the heart. In reality, whenever you are in love you are relaxed, and because you are relaxed you are filled with a certain peace. That peace arises from the heart.

So peace and love have become joined, associated. Whenever you are in love you are peaceful; whenever you are not in love you are disturbed. Because of peace, the heart has become associated with love.

So you can do two things. You can search for love, then sometimes you will feel peace. But this path is dangerous, because the other person whom you love has become more important than you. And the other is the other, and you are becoming in a way dependent. So love will give you peace sometimes but not always. There will be many disturbances, many moments of anguish and anxiety, because the other has entered your world. Whenever another enters, there is bound to be some disturbance, because you can meet with the other only on the surface. The surface will be disturbed. Only sometimes, when the two of you are deeply in love, with no conflict – only then will you sometimes be relaxed and the heart will glow with peace.

So love can give you glimpses of peace but nothing really established, rooted. No eternal peace is possible through it, only glimpses. And between two glimpses there will be valleys of conflict, violence, hatred and anger.

The other way is to find peace not through love, but directly. If you can find peace directly – and this is the method for it – your life will become filled with love. But the quality of this love will be different. It will not be possessive; it will not be centred on one person. It will not be dependent and it will not make anyone dependent on you. Your love will become just a lovingness, a compassion, a deep empathy. And then no one, not even a lover, can disturb you because your peace is already rooted within you, and your love comes as a shadow of your inner peace. The whole thing has turned around.

So Buddha loves, but his love does not involve anguish. If you love you will suffer, and if you don't love you will suffer. If you don't love you will suffer the absence of love; if you love you will suffer the presence of love. Because you are on the surface and whatever you do can only give you momentary satisfaction – then the dark valley appears again.

First be established in peace on your own. Then you are independent, then love is not your 'need'. Then you will never feel imprisoned when you are in love; you will never feel that love has become a sort of dependence, a slavery, a bondage. Then love will be just a giving: you will have so much peace that you will want to share it. Then it will be just a giving with no idea of return; it will be unconditional. And it is one of the secrets that the more you give, the more it happens to you. The more you give and share, the more it becomes your own. The deeper you enter into the treasury, which is infinite, the more you can go on giving to everybody. It is inexhaustible.

But love must happen to you as a shadow of inner peace. Ordinarily the reverse is what happens: peace comes to you just as a shadow of love. When love happens to you as a shadow of peace, then love is beautiful. Otherwise love also creates ugliness, it becomes a disease, a fever.

... pervade an area between the armpits into great peace.

Become aware of the area between the armpits and feel that it is filled with great peace. Just feel peace there and you will feel that it is filled. It is always filled but you have never been aware of it. This is only to increase your alertness, to bring you nearer home. And when you feel this peace, you are further away from the surface. Not that things won't be happening there – but when you try this experiment and when you are filled with peace, you will feel distant from it. The noise is coming from the street but there is a great distance now, a great space. It happens, but it brings no disturbance; rather, it brings you a deeper silence. This is the miracle. The children will be playing, someone will be listening to the radio, people will be quarrelling and the whole world will be going on around you, but you feel that a great distance has come between you and everything outside. That distance arises because you have retreated from the periphery. Things are happening on the periphery and they will appear to you as if they are happening somewhere else. You are not involved. Nothing disturbs you, so you are not involved – you have transcended. This is transcendence.

And the heart is naturally the source of peace. You are not creating anything. You are simply coming to a source that is always there. This imagining will help you become aware that the heart is filled with peace – it is not that the imagining will create the peace. This is the difference between the Eastern attitude and Western hypnosis. Hypnotists think that you are creating it with your imagination but the Eastern mystic knows that you are not creating it with your imagination, you are simply becoming attuned to something that is already there.

Whatever you can create through your imagination cannot be permanent: if it is not a reality then it is false, unreal, and you are just creating a hallucination. It is better to be disturbed and real than to be in a hallucination of peace, because that is not growth. You are simply intoxicated by it. Sooner or later you will have to come out of it because sooner or later the reality will shatter the illusion. Reality has to shatter all illusions; only a greater reality cannot be shattered.

A greater reality will shatter the reality that is on the periphery; hence Shankara and other Eastern philosophers say that the world is illusion. Not that the world is illusion, but

...if the world has become a dream then dreams cannot continue.

they have come to know a higher reality and from that altitude this world looks dreamlike. It is so far away, the distance is so infinite that it cannot be felt as real. The noise on the street will be as if you are dreaming about it – it is not real. It cannot do anything to you. It just happens and passes by and you remain untouched. And when you are untouched by reality, how can you feel that it is real? The reality is felt only when it penetrates you deeply. The deeper the penetration, the more you feel it as real.

Shankara says the whole world is unreal. He must have come to a point where the distance was so vast, so tremendously vast, that all that happened outside became just like a dream. The world was around him, but it seemed unreal because it could not penetrate him. Penetration is the measure of reality. If I throw a stone at you, it hits you. The hit penetrates you and that penetration makes the stone real. If I throw a stone and it touches you but doesn't penetrate you, deep down you will hear the thud of the stone falling on you, but there will be no disturbance. You will feel it as false, unreal, illusory.

But you are so near the periphery that if I throw a stone at you, you will be hurt. I'm not talking about the body – the body will be hurt in either case. If I throw a stone at Buddha, his body will be hurt as your body will be hurt. But Buddha is not on the periphery, he is rooted at the centre. And the distance is so great that he will hear the thud of the stone without being hurt. The being will remain untouched, unscarred. This unscarred being will feel the stone as if it is something thrown in a dream. So Buddha says that nothing has substance to it, everything is 'without substance'. The world is empty of substance – which is the same thing as Shankara saying that the world is illusory.

Try this. Whenever you are able to feel the peace between your two armpits filling you, pervading your heart centre, the world will look illusory. This is a sign that you have entered meditation – when the world feels and appears to be illusory. Don't think that the world is illusory, there is no need to think it – you will feel it. It will suddenly occur to you, 'What has happened to the world?' The world has suddenly become dreamlike. It is there, a dreamlike existence without any substance. It looks so real, just like a film on the screen. It can even be three-dimensional. It looks like something, but it is a projected thing.

Not that the world is really a projected thing, not that it is truly unreal – no. The

And if the world is unreal, you are totally relaxed...

world is real – but you can create a distance, and the distance grows greater and greater. And you can understand whether the distance is getting greater or not by knowing how you are feeling about the world. That's the criterion. That is a meditative criterion. It is not a truth that the world is unreal – but if the world has become unreal to you, you have become centred in your being. Now the distance between you and the surface is so great that you can look at the surface as being something objective, something other than you. You are not identified.

This technique is very easy and will not take much time. It sometimes happens that at the very first attempt people feel the beauty and the miracle of it. So try it. But if you don't feel anything at the first attempt, don't be disappointed. Wait. And go on doing it. It is so easy that you can go on doing it any time. Just lying on your bed at night you can do it; in the morning when you feel that you are now awake you can do it. Do it first and then get up. Even ten minutes will be enough. Do it for ten minutes at night just before falling asleep. Make the world unreal, and your sleep will be so deep that you may not have ever slept like that before. If the world becomes unreal just before falling asleep, your dreaming will be less. Because if the world

has become a dream then dreams cannot continue. And if the world is unreal, you are totally relaxed because the reality of the world will not impinge on you, hammer on you.

This technique is good for people who suffer from insomnia. It helps greatly. If the world is unreal, tensions dissolve. If you can move away from the periphery, you have already moved to a deep state of sleep – before sleep comes you are already deep into it. And then in the morning it is beautiful because you are so fresh, so young; your whole energy vibrates. It is because you are coming back to the periphery from the centre.

The moment you become alert once sleep is no more, don't open your eyes. First do this experiment for ten minutes, then open the eyes. The body is relaxed after the whole night and is feeling fresh and alive. You are already relaxed, so it will not take much time. Just relax. Bring your consciousness to the heart just between the two armpits: feel it filled with deep peace. For ten minutes remain in that peace, then open the eyes.

The world will look totally different because that peace will also be radiated from your eyes. And the whole day you will feel different – not only will you feel different but also you will feel that people are behaving differently towards you.

To every relationship you contribute something. If your contribution changes, people behave differently because they feel you are a different person. They may not be aware of it. But when you are filled with peace everyone will behave differently towards you. They will be more loving and more kind, less resistant, more open, closer. A magnet is there. Peace is the magnet.

When you are peaceful, people come nearer to you; when you are disturbed everyone is repelled. And this is so physical a phenomenon that you can observe it easily. Whenever you are peaceful you will feel everyone wants to be closer to you because that peace radiates, it becomes a vibration around you. Circles of peace move around you and whoever comes near wants to be nearer to you – as if they want to move under the shade of a tree and relax there.

A person who is peaceful within has a shade around him. Wherever he goes everyone would like to be closer to him, more open, trusting. A person who has inner turmoil, conflict, anguish, anxiety, tensions, repels others. Whoever comes near that person becomes afraid; he is dangerous. To be near him is dangerous.

Because you will give whatever you have, you are constantly giving it. So you may want to love someone but if you are very disturbed within, even your lover will be repelled and will want to escape from you because you will drain his energy and he will not feel happy with you. And whenever you leave him, you will leave him tired,

exhausted, because you don't have a life-giving source; you have a destructive energy within you.

So not only will you feel you are different, others will also feel that you are different.

Your whole lifestyle can change if you move a little closer to the centre – as will your whole outlook and the whole outcome of your activities. If you are peaceful, the whole world becomes peaceful towards you. It is just a reflection. Whatever you are is reflected all over. Everyone becomes a mirror.

Remember, you can give to others only that which you have. If you are miserable, regardless of what you say or do you will make others miserable. If you are blissful, you need not say anything – you will make others blissful. Your very presence will trigger some blissfulness in their being. Your very presence will create a synchronicity in others. Your music, your dance, will create ripples of joy – whoever is close to you will become infected with your joy.

his story/her story

i t is one of the strangest phenomena that for thousands of years men and women have been living together, yet they are strangers. They go on having children, but still they remain strangers. The feminine approach and the masculine approach are so opposed to each other that unless a conscious effort is made, unless it becomes your meditation, there is no hope of having a peaceful life.

It is one of my deep concerns: how to make love and meditation so involved in each other that each love affair automatically becomes a partnership in meditation – and each meditation makes you so conscious that you need not fall in love, you can rise in love. You can find a friend consciously, deliberately.

Your love will deepen as your meditation deepens, and vice-versa: as your meditation blossoms, your love will also blossom. But it is on a totally different level.

With your husband, you are not connected in meditation. You never sit silently for one hour together just to feel each other's consciousness. Either you are fighting or you are making love, but in both cases, you are related with the body, the physical part, the biology, the hormones. You are not related with the innermost core of the other. Your souls remain separate.

In the temples and in the churches and in the courts, only your bodies are married.

...as your meditation blossoms, your love will also blossom.

Your souls are miles apart. While you are making love to your partner – even in those moments – neither you nor your partner is there. Perhaps he is thinking of Cleopatra, Helen of Troy, some movie starlet. You are also thinking of somebody else. Perhaps that's why every woman keeps her eyes closed – so as not to see her husband's face, not to get disturbed. She is thinking of Alexander the Great, Ivan the Terrible, and looking at her husband, so everything falls apart. He looks just like a mouse.

Even in those beautiful moments, which should be sacred, meditative, of deep silence ... even then you are not alone with your beloved. There is a crowd. Your mind is thinking of somebody else, your wife's mind is thinking of somebody else. Then what you are doing is just robot-like, mechanical. Some biological force is enslaving you, and you call it love.

I have heard that early in the morning, a drunkard on the beach saw a man doing push-ups. The drunkard walked around him, looked very closely from here and from there, and finally said, 'I should not interfere in such an intimate affair, but I have to tell you that your girlfriend has gone. Now don't exercise unnecessarily – first get up and find where she is!'

That seems to be the situation. When you are making love, is your woman really there? Is your man really there? Or are you just taking part in a ritual – something that has to be done, just a duty to be fulfilled?

If you want a harmonious relationship with your partner, you will have to learn to be more meditative. Love alone is not enough. Love alone is blind; meditation gives it eyes. Meditation gives it understanding. And once your love is both love and meditation, you become fellow travellers. Then it is no longer an ordinary relationship between two people. Then it becomes a friendliness on the path towards discovering the mysteries of life.

Man alone, woman alone, will find the journey very tedious and very long ... as they have found it in the past.

Seeing this continuous conflict, all the religions decided that those who wanted to follow the spiritual path should renounce the other – that monks should be celibate, that nuns should be celibate.

But in five thousand years of history, how many monks and how many nuns have become realized souls? You cannot even find names enough to count on ten fingers. And there have been millions of monks and nuns of all religions – Buddhist, Hindu, Christian, Muslim. What has happened?

The path is not so long. The goal is not that far away. But even if you want to go to your neighbour's house, you will need both your legs. Just hopping on one leg, how far can you go?

Men and women together in deep friendship, in a loving, meditative relationship, as organic wholes, can reach the goal any moment they want. Because the goal is not outside you; it is the centre of the cyclone, it is the innermost part of your being. But you can find it only when you are whole, and you cannot be whole without the other.

Man and woman are two parts, two aspects of one whole.

So rather than wasting time in fighting, try to understand each other. Try to put yourself in the place of the other; try to see as a man sees, try to see as a woman sees. And four eyes are always better than two eyes – you have a full view; all four directions are available to you.

But one thing has to be remembered: that without meditation, love is destined to fail; there is no possibility of it succeeding. You can pretend and you can deceive others, but you cannot deceive yourself. You know deep down that all the promises love has given to you have remained unfulfilled.

Only with meditation does love start taking on new colours, new music, new songs, new dances – because meditation gives you the insight to understand the polar opposite, and in that very understanding the conflict disappears.

All the conflict in the world is because of misunderstanding. You say something, your wife hears something else. Your wife says something, you hear something else.

I have seen couples who have lived together for 30 or 40 years; still, they seem to be as immature as they were on their first day together. Still the same complaint: 'She doesn't understand what I am saying.' Forty years of being together and you have not been able to figure out some way for your wife to understand exactly what you are saying, and for you to understand exactly what she is saying.

I think there is no possibility for it to happen except through meditation, because meditation gives you the qualities of silence, awareness, a patient listening, a capacity to put yourself in the other's position.

Things are not impossible, but we have not tried the right medicine.

I would like you to be reminded that the word 'medicine' comes from the same root as 'meditation'. Medicine cures your body; meditation cures your soul. Medicine heals the material part of you; meditation heals the spiritual part of you.

People are living together and their spirits are full of wounds; hence, small things hurt them so much.

Mulla Nasruddin was asking me, 'What should I do? Whatever I say I am misunderstood, and immediately there is trouble.'

I said, 'Try one thing: just sit silently, don't say anything.'

The next day, I saw him in more despair than ever. I said, 'What happened?'

He said, 'I should not ask you for advice. Every day we used to fight and quarrel, but it was just verbal. Yesterday, because of your advice, I got beaten!'

I said, 'What happened?'

He said, 'I just sat there silently. She asked me many questions, but I was determined to remain silent. She said, "So you are not going to speak?" I remained silent. So she started hitting me with things! She said, "Things have gone from bad to worse. At least we used to talk to each other; now we are not even on speaking terms!"'

I said, 'This is really bad.'

He said, 'You say it's bad? The whole neighbourhood gathered, and they all started asking, "What's happened? Why aren't you speaking?" And somebody suggested: "It seems he is possessed by an evil spirit."'

'I thought, my God, now they are going to take me to some idiot who will beat me and try to drive the evil spirit out. I said, "Wait! I'm not possessed by any evil spirit, I'm simply not speaking because anything I say triggers a fight. I say something, then she has to say something, and then I have to say something, and nobody knows where it is going to end." I was simply meditating silently, doing no harm to anybody – and suddenly the whole neighbourhood was against me!'

People are living without any understanding. Hence, whatever they do is going to end in disaster.

If you love a man, meditation will be the best present that you can give to him. If you love a woman, then a diamond ring is nothing; meditation will be a far more precious gift – and it will make your life sheer joy.

We are potentially capable of sheer joy, but we don't know how to manage it. Alone, we are at the most sad. Together, it becomes really hell!

Even a man like Jean-Paul Sartre, a man of great intelligence, has to say that the other is hell, that to be alone is better, you cannot make it with the other. He became so pessimistic that he said it is impossible to make it with the other, the other is hell. Ordinarily, he is right.

With meditation the other becomes your heaven. But Jean-Paul Sartre had no idea of meditation.

That is the misery of Western people. Western people are missing the flowering of life because they know nothing about meditation, and Eastern people are missing the flowering of life because they know nothing of love.

And to me, just as man and woman are halves of one whole, so are love and meditation. Meditation is man; love is woman. In the meeting of meditation and love is the meeting of man and woman. And in that meeting, we create the transcendental human being – which is neither man nor woman.

Unless we create the transcendental human being on the earth, there is not much hope.

lovemaking as a meditation

tantra has always been misunderstood. It cannot be understood by ordinary people; they are bound to misunderstand it. It is a form of prayer, it has nothing to do with sex. Even making love has nothing to do with sex. When it becomes a meditation, a prayer – just the melting and meeting and merging of energies in a prayerful mood – it is not even just fun or playfulness, it is devotion.

This is a Tantric technique for approaching lovemaking as a meditation.

While being caressed, enter the caress as everlasting life.

This technique is concerned with love, because love is the nearest thing in your experience during which you are relaxed. If you cannot love, it is impossible for you to relax. If you can relax, your life will become a loving life.

A tense person cannot love. Why? A tense person always lives with purposes. A tense person can earn money, but she cannot love because love is purposeless. Love is not a commodity. You cannot accumulate it; you cannot create a bank balance of it; you cannot strengthen your ego out of it. Really, love is the most absurd act, with no meaning beyond it, no purpose beyond it. It exists for itself, not for anything else.

You earn money for something – it is a means. You build a house for someone to live in – it is a means. Love is not a means.

While being caressed, enter the caress as everlasting life.

Why do you love? For what do you love? Love is the end in itself. That is why a mind that is calculating, logical, a mind that thinks in terms of purpose, cannot love. And the mind that always thinks in terms of purpose will be tense, because purpose can only be fulfilled in the future, never here and now. You are building a house – you cannot live in it right now, you will have to build it first. You can live in it in the future, not now. You earn money – the bank balance will be created in the future, not now. The means are in the present, and the ends will come in the future.

Love is always here; there is no future to it. That is why love is so near to meditation. That is why death is also so near to meditation – because death is always in the here and now; it can never happen in the future. Can you die in the future? You can die only in the present. No one has ever died in the future. How can you die in the future? Or how can you die in the past? The past has gone, it is no more, so you cannot die in it. Death always occurs in the present. Death, love, meditation – they all occur in the present. So if you are afraid of death, you cannot love. If you are afraid of love, you cannot meditate. If you are afraid of meditation, your life will be useless. Useless not in the sense of any purpose, but useless in

the sense that you will never be able to feel any bliss in it. It will be futile.

It may seem strange to connect these three: love, meditation, death. It is not! They are similar experiences. So if you can enter into one, you can enter into the remaining two.

This technique is concerned with love. It says, 'While being caressed, enter the caress as everlasting life.' What does it mean? Many things! One: while you are being loved the past has ceased, the future does not exist. You move in the dimension of the present. You move in the now.

Have you ever loved someone? If you have ever loved, then you know that the mind is no longer there. That is why the so-called wise men say that lovers are blind, mindless, mad. In essence what they say is right. Lovers are blind because they have no eyes for the future, to calculate what they are going to do. They are blind; they cannot see the past. What has happened to lovers? They just move in the here and now without any consideration of past or future, without any consideration of consequences. That is why they are called blind. They are! To those who are calculating, they are blind – and for those who are not calculating, they are seers. Those who are not calculating will see love as real sight, real vision.

So the first thing is that in the moment of love, past and future are no more. Then, one delicate point is to be understood. When there is no past and no future, can you call this moment the present? The present exists only between the two – between the past and the future. It is relative. If there is no past and no future, what does it mean to talk about the present? It is meaningless. That is why Shiva doesn't use the word present. He says, 'everlasting life'. He means eternity ... you enter eternity.

We divide time into three parts – past, present, future. That division is false, absolutely false. Time is really past and future. The present is not part of time.

The present is part of eternity. That which has passed is time; that which is to come is time. That which is now is not time because it never passes – it is always here. The now is always here. It is always here! This now is eternal.

If you move from the past, you never move into the present. From the past you always move into the future; there comes no moment that is present. From the present you can never move into the future. From the present you go deeper and deeper, into more present and more present. This is everlasting life.

We may say it in this way: from past to future is time. Time means you move on a plane, on a straight line. Or we can call it horizontal. The moment you are in the present the dimension changes: you move vertically – up or down, towards the heights or towards the depths. But then you never move horizontally. A Buddha and a Shiva live in eternity, not in time.

Jesus was asked, 'What will happen in your kingdom of God?' The man who asked him was not asking about time. He was asking about what is going to happen to his desires, about how they will be fulfilled. He was asking whether there will be life everlasting or whether there will be death; whether there be any misery, whether there will be inferior and superior people. He was asking about things of this world when he asked, 'What is going to happen in your kingdom of God?' And Jesus replied – the reply is like that of a Zen monk – 'There shall be time no longer.'

The man who received this response may not have understood what was meant by 'There shall be time no longer'. Jesus said 'There shall be time no longer' because time is horizontal and the kingdom of God is vertical ... it is eternal. It is always here! You have only to move away from time to enter into it.

So love is the first door. Through it, you can move away from time. That is why everyone wants to be loved, everyone wants to love. And no one knows why so much significance is given to love, why there is such a deep longing for love. And unless you know it rightly, you can neither love nor be loved, because love is one of the deepest phenomena upon this earth.

We go on thinking that everyone is capable of love just as he or she is. This is not the case – it is not so. That is why you are frustrated. Love is a different dimension, and if you try to love someone in time you will be defeated in your effort. In time, love is not possible.

I look in front of me and there is a wall; I move my eyes and there is the sky. When you look in time there is always a wall. When you look beyond time there is the open sky ... infinite. Love opens the infinity, the everlastingness of existence. So really, if you have ever loved, love can be made a technique of meditation. This is the technique: while being loved, enter loving as everlasting life.

Do not be a lover standing aloof, outside. Become loving and move into eternity. When you are loving someone, are you there as

the lover? If you are there, then you are in time and love is just false. If you are still there and you can say, 'I am', then you can be physically near but spiritually you are poles apart.

While in love, you must not be – only love, only loving. Become loving. While caressing your lover or beloved, become the caress. While kissing, do not be the kisser or the kissed – be the kiss. Forget the ego completely, dissolve it into the act. Move into the act so deeply that the actor is no more. And if you cannot move into love, it is difficult to move into eating or walking – very difficult, because love is the easiest approach for dissolving the ego. That is why those who are egoists cannot love. They may talk about it, they may sing about it, they may write about it, but they cannot love. The ego cannot love!

Become loving. When you are in the embrace, become the embrace, become the kiss. Forget yourself so totally that you can say, 'I am no more. Only love exists.' Then the heart is not beating but love is beating. Then the blood is not circulating, love is circulating. And the eyes are not seeing, love is seeing. Then hands are not moving to touch, love is moving to touch.

Become love and enter everlasting life. Love suddenly changes your dimension. You are thrown out of time and you are

Tantra means this: the transformation of love into meditation.

facing eternity. Love can become a deep meditation – the deepest possible. Lovers have known sometimes what saints have not known. And lovers have touched that centre that many yogis have missed. But it will be just a glimpse unless you transform your love into meditation. Tantra means this: the transformation of love into meditation. And now you can understand why Tantra talks so much about love and sex. Why? Because love is the easiest natural door from which you can transcend this world, this horizontal dimension.

Look at the pictures from the East of the Lord Shiva with his consort, Devi. Look at them! They don't appear to be two – they are one. The oneness is so deep that it has even gone into symbols. We have all seen the Shivalinga. It is a phallic symbol – Shiva's sex organ – but it is not alone, it is based in Devi's vagina. The Hindus of the old days were very daring. Now when you see a Shivalinga you never remember that it is a phallic symbol. We have forgotten; we have tried to forget it completely.

Carl Jung remembers in his autobiography, in his memoirs, a very beautiful and funny incident. He came to India and went to see Konark, and in the temple of Konark there are many, many Shivalingas, many phallic symbols. The pundit who was taking him around explained everything to him except the Shivalingas. And they were so many, it was difficult to escape them. Jung was well aware of the situation, but just to tease the pundit he went on asking, 'But what are these?' So the pundit at last said into his ear, in Jung's ear, 'Do not ask me here, I will tell you afterwards. This is a private thing.'

Jung must have laughed inside – these are the Hindus of today. Then outside the temple the pundit came near and said, 'It was not good of you to ask in front of others. I will tell you now. It is a secret.' And then again in Jung's ear he said, 'They are our private parts.'

When Jung went back to Europe, he met a great scholar – a scholar of oriental thought, mythology and philosophy, Heinrich Zimmer. He related this anecdote to Zimmer. Zimmer was one of the most gifted minds that ever tried to penetrate Indian thought and he was a lover of India and of its ways of thinking – of the oriental, non-logical, mystic approach towards life. When he heard this from Jung, he laughed and said, 'This makes a change. I have always heard about great Indians – Buddha, Krishna, Mahavir. What you relate says something not about any great Indians, but about Indians.'

Love is the great gate. And for Tantra, sex is not something to be condemned. For Tantra, sex is the seed and love is the flowering of it, and if you condemn the seed you condemn the flower. Sex can become love. If it never becomes love then it is crippled. Condemn the fact that it is crippled, not the sex. Love must flower, sex must become love. If it does not become love, it is not the fault of sex, it is your fault.

Sex must not remain sex; that is the Tantric teaching. It must be transformed into love. And love also must not remain love. It must be transformed into light, into meditative experience. How to transform love? Be the act and forget the actor. While loving, be love – simply love. Then it is not your love or my love or anybody else's – it is simply love. When you are not there, when you are in the hands of the ultimate source, or current, when you are in love, it is not you who is in love. When the love has engulfed you, you have disappeared; you have just become a flowing energy.

D. H. Lawrence, one of the most creative minds of this age, was knowingly or unknowingly a Tantra adept. He was condemned in the West completely and his books were banned. There were many court cases over his words because he had said, 'Sex energy is the only energy, and if you condemn it and suppress it you are against the universe. Then you will never be capable of knowing the higher flowering of this energy. And when it is suppressed it becomes ugly – this is the vicious circle.'

Priests, moralists and other so-called religious people go on condemning sex. They say that it is an ugly thing. And when you suppress it, then it does indeed become ugly. So they say, 'Look! What we said is true. You have proved it.' But it is not sex that is ugly, it is these priests who have made it ugly. Once they have made it ugly they are proved right. And when they are proved right, you go on making it more and more ugly.

Sex is innocent energy – life flowing in you, existence alive in you. Do not cripple it! Allow it to move towards the heights. That is, sex must become love. What is the difference? When your mind is sexual you are exploiting the other; the other is just an instrument to be used and thrown away. When sex becomes love the other is not an instrument, the other is not to be exploited; the other is not really the other. When you love, it is not self-centred. Rather, the other becomes significant, unique.

It is not that you are exploiting him – no! On the contrary, you are both joined in a deep experience. You are partners in a deep experience, not the exploiter and the exploited. You are helping each other to move into a different world of love. Sex is exploitation. Love is moving together into a different world.

If this moving is not momentary and if this moving becomes meditative – that is, if you can forget yourself completely and the lover and the beloved disappear, and there is only love flowing – then, says Tantra, everlasting life is yours.

part four

meditations for
everyday life

In the past this has been one of the fallacies: you meditate for 20 minutes, or you meditate three times a day, or you meditate five times a day – the basic idea is that a few minutes every day should be given to meditation. But what are you going to do in the remaining 23 hours and 40 minutes? No doubt something anti-meditative. Naturally, whatever you gained in the 20 minutes will be lost during the remaining time in the day.

I want you to look at meditation from a totally different standpoint. You can learn meditation for 20 minutes or 40 minutes – learning is one thing – but then you have to carry out whatever you have learned day in, day out. Meditation has to become just like your heartbeat.

natural and easy

Whenever you find time, relax the breathing system just for a few minutes, but nothing else – there is no need to relax the whole body. Sitting in the train or plane, or in the car, nobody will become aware that you are doing something. Just relax the breathing system. Let it be just as it is when it is functioning naturally. Then close your eyes and watch the breathing going in, coming out, going in ...

Don't concentrate! If you concentrate, you create trouble, because then everything becomes a disturbance. If you try to concentrate sitting in the car, then the noise of the car becomes a disturbance, the person sitting beside you becomes a disturbance.

Meditation is not concentration. It is simple awareness. You simply relax and watch the breathing. In that watching, nothing is excluded. The car is humming – perfectly okay, accept it. The traffic is passing – that's okay, part of life. The fellow passenger snoring by your side, accept it. Nothing is rejected.

You cannot avoid truth. It is better to face it, it is better to accept it, it is better to live it. Once you start living a life of truth and authenticity, all troubles start to disappear because conflict disappears and you are no longer divided. Your voice now has a unity, your whole being becomes an orchestra. Right now, when you say something, your body says something else; when your tongue says something, your eyes go on saying something else simultaneously.

People often come to me and I ask them, 'How are you?' And they say, 'We are very, very happy.' And I cannot believe it because their faces are so dull – no joy, no delight! Their eyes have no shine to them, no light. And when they say, 'We are happy,' even the word 'happy' does not sound very happy. It sounds as if they are dragging it out.

Their tone, their voice, their face, the way they are sitting or standing – everything belies it, says something else.

Start watching people. When they say that they are happy, watch. Watch for a clue. Are they really happy? And immediately you will be aware that some part of them is saying something else. And then, by and by, watch yourself. When you are saying that you are happy and you are not, there will be a disturbance in your breathing. Your breathing cannot be natural. It is impossible. Because the truth was that you were not happy. If you had said, 'I am unhappy,' your breathing would have remained natural. There was no conflict. But you said, 'I am happy.' Immediately you are repressing something – something that was coming up, you have forced down. In this very effort your breathing changes its rhythm; it is no longer rhythmical. Your face is no longer graceful, your eyes become deceiving.

First watch others because it will be easier to do. You can be more objective about them. And when you have found clues about them, use the same clues about yourself. And see – when you speak truth, your voice has a musical tone to it; when you speak untruth, something is there like a jarring note. When you speak truth you are one, together; when you speak untruth you are not together, a conflict has arisen. Watch these subtle phenomena, because they are the consequence of togetherness or untogetherness.

Whenever you are together, not falling apart; whenever you are one, in unison, suddenly you will see you are happy. That is the meaning of the word 'yoga'. That's what we mean by a yogi: one who is together, in unison; whose parts are all interrelated and not contradictory; they are interdependent, not in conflict, at peace with each other. A great friendship exists within his being. He is whole.

Sometimes it happens that you become one, in a rare moment. Watch the ocean, the tremendous wildness of it – and suddenly you forget your split, your schizophrenia; you relax. Or, moving in the Himalayas, seeing the virgin snow on the Himalayan peaks, suddenly a coolness surrounds you and you need not be false because there is no other human being to whom you can be false. You fall together. Or, listening to beautiful music, you fall together.

Whenever, in whatever situation, you find yourself becoming one, a peace, a happiness, a bliss, surrounds you, arises in you. You feel fulfilled.

There is no need to wait for these moments – these moments can become your natural life. These extraordinary moments can become ordinary moments – that is the whole point of Zen. You can live an extraordinary life in a very ordinary life: cutting wood, chopping wood, carrying water from the well, you can be tremendously at ease with yourself. Cleaning the floor, cooking food, washing the clothes, you can be perfectly at ease – because the whole question is about you doing your action totally, enjoying it, delighting in it.

breath is a key

Watch a child; that is the right way to breathe. When a child breathes, the chest is completely unaffected. The belly goes up and down. The child breathes as if from the belly. All children have a little belly; that belly is there because of their breathing and the reservoir of energy.

That is the right way to breathe. Remember not to use your chest too much; it is to be used only rarely – in times of emergency. If you are running to save your life, then the chest can be used. It is an emergency device. Then you can use shallow, fast breathing, and run. But ordinarily the chest should not be used. And one thing to remember: the chest is meant only for emergency situations because it is difficult in an emergency situation to breathe naturally. If you breathe naturally you remain so calm and quiet you cannot run, you cannot fight; you are so calm and collected, you are like a buddha. And in an emergency – for example, the house is on fire – if you breathe naturally you will not be able to save anything. Or if a tiger jumps upon you in a forest, and you go on breathing naturally, you will not be bothered; it is as if you are saying, 'Okay, let him do whatever he wants'. You will not be able to protect yourself.

So nature has provided an emergency device; the chest is an emergency device. When a tiger attacks you, you have to drop natural breathing and you have to breathe from the chest. Then you will have more capacity to run, to fight, to burn energy fast. And in an emergency situation there are only two alternatives – flight or fight. Both need a very shallow but intense energy, shallow but a very disturbed, tense state.

Now if you continuously breathe from the chest, you will have tensions in your mind. If you continuously breathe from the chest, you will always be afraid. Because chest breathing is meant to be used only in situations of fear. And if you have made a habit of it, then you will be continuously afraid, tense, always ready for flight. The enemy is not there, but you will imagine the enemy is there. That's how paranoia is created.

In the West a few people have come across this phenomenon, such as Alexander Lowen and others who have worked on bio-energetics. They have come to feel that in people who are afraid, the chest is tense, and they take very shallow breaths. If their breathing can be made deeper, so that it goes and touches the belly, the hara centre, then their fear disappears. Ida Rolf has invented one of the most beautiful methods of changing the inner structure of the body – Rolfing. If you have been breathing wrongly for many years, you will have developed a certain musculature, and that musculature will be in the way and will not allow you to breathe deeply. And even if you remember to breathe deeply for a few seconds, once you are engaged in your work again, you will start breathing shallowly, in the chest.

The musculature has to be changed. Once the musculature has changed, the fear disappears and the tension disappears.

Watch a child breathe – that is the natural way of breathing – and breathe that way. Let your belly come up when you inhale, let your belly go down when you exhale. And let it be in such a rhythm that it becomes almost a song of your energy, a dance with rhythm, with harmony – and you will feel so relaxed, so alive, so vital that you cannot imagine that such vitality is possible.

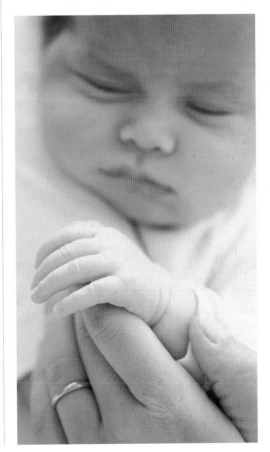

relaxed attention

In his Vigyan Bhairav Tantra, Shiva gives this meditation technique: Wherever your attention alights, at this very point, experience.

In this technique, firstly you have to develop attention. You have to develop an attentive kind of attitude. Only then will this technique become possible, so that wherever your attention alights you can experience – you can experience yourself. Just by looking at a flower you can experience yourself. Then looking at a flower is not just looking at the flower, but at the looker also – but only if you know the secret of attention.

You may look at a flower and think you are looking at the flower, but you have started thinking about the flower, and the flower is missed. You are no longer there, you have gone somewhere else, you have moved away. Attention means that when you are looking at a flower, you are looking at a flower and not doing anything else – as if the mind has stopped, as if now there is no thinking and only a simple experience of the flower is there. You are here, the flower is there, and between you two there is no thought.

If you can do this, you will find that suddenly, from the flower, your attention will come back, bounce back to you. It will become a circle. You will look at the flower and the look will come back. The flower will reflect it, bounce it back to you. If there are

You are here, the flower is there ... between you two there is no thought.

no thoughts, this happens. Then you are not looking only at the flower, you are looking at the looker also. Then the looker and the flower have become two objects and you have become a witness of both.

But first, attention has to be trained, because you have no attention at all. Your attention is just flickering, moving from this to that, from that to something else. Not for a single moment are you attentive. Even when I am talking, you never hear all my words. You hear one word, then your attention goes somewhere else; then you come back, you hear another, then your attention goes somewhere else. You hear a few words, and you fill in the gaps, and then you think you have heard me. Whatever you carry with yourself, it is your own business; it is your own creation. You have heard just a few words from me, and then you have filled in the gaps, and whatever you put in the gaps changes everything! I say a word, and you have started thinking about it. You cannot remain silent.

If you can remain silent while hearing, you will become attentive.

Attention means a silent alertness with no thoughts interfering. Develop it. You can develop it only by doing it; there is no other way. Do it more and you will develop it.

Whatever you are doing, wherever you are, try to develop it.

You are travelling in a car, or on a train. What are you doing there? Try to develop attention; don't waste time. For half an hour you will be on a train: develop attention. Just be there. Don't think. Look at someone, look at the train or look outside, but be the look, don't think anything. Stop thinking. Be there and look. Your look will become direct, penetrating, and from everywhere your look will be reflected back and you will become aware of the looker.

You are not aware of yourself because there is a wall. When you look at a flower, first your thoughts change your look; they give their own colour. Then that look goes to the flower. It comes back, but then again your thoughts give it a different colour. And when it comes back it never finds you there. You have moved somewhere else, you are not there.

Every look comes back; everything is reflected, responded to, but you are not there to receive it. So be there to receive it. During a whole day you can try this out on many things, and by and by you will develop attentiveness. With that attentiveness do this:

Wherever your attention alights, at this very point, experience.

Then look anywhere, but simply look. The attention has alighted – and you will experience yourself. But the first requirement is to have the capacity to be attentive. And you can practise it. There is no need for it to take up extra time.

Whatever you are doing – eating, taking a bath, standing under a shower – just be attentive. But what is the problem? The problem is that we do everything with the mind, and we are planning continuously for the future. You may be travelling on a train, but your mind may be arranging other journeys; programming, planning. Stop this.

One Zen monk, Bokuju, said, 'This is the only meditation I know. While I eat, I eat. While I walk, I walk. And when I feel sleepy, I sleep. Whatever happens, happens. I never interfere.'

That's all there is to it – don't interfere. And whatever happens, allow it to happen; simply be there. That will give you attentiveness. And when you have attention, this technique is just in your hand.

Wherever your attention alights, at this very point, experience.

You will experience the experiencer; you will fall back to yourself. From everywhere you will be rebounded; from everywhere you will be reflected. The whole of existence will become a mirror; you will be reflected everywhere. The whole of existence will mirror you, and only then can you know yourself, not before.

Unless the whole of existence becomes a mirror for you, unless every part of existence

The whole of existence will become a mirror; you will be reflected everywhere.

reveals you, unless every relationship opens you ... You are such an infinite phenomenon – ordinary mirrors won't do. You are such a vast existence within that unless the whole of existence becomes a mirror you will not be able to get a glimpse. When the whole universe becomes a mirror, only then will you be mirrored. In you exists the divine.

And the technique to make existence a mirror is this: create attention, become more alert, and then wherever your attention alights – wherever, on any object – suddenly experience yourself. This is possible, but right now it is impossible because you don't fulfil the basic requirements.

You can look at a flower, but that is not attention. You are just running near the flower, around and around. You have seen the flower while running; you have not been there for a single moment.

Wherever your attention alights, at this very point, experience.

Just remember yourself.

There is a deep reason why this technique can be helpful. You can throw a ball and hit a wall – the ball will come back. When you look at a flower or at a face, a certain energy is being thrown out – your look is energy. And you are not aware that when you look, you are investing some energy, you are throwing out some energy. A certain quantity of your life energy is being thrown out. That's why you feel exhausted after looking at the

streets all day: at the people passing, advertisements, the crowd, the shops. Looking at everything makes you feel exhausted, and then you want to close your eyes, to relax. Why are you feeling so exhausted? You have been throwing out energy.

Buddha and Mahavir both insisted that their monks should not look too much; they must concentrate on the ground. Buddha says that you can only look up to a metre ahead. Don't look anywhere; just look at the path where you are moving. To look one metre ahead is enough, because when you have moved one metre, you will again be looking one metre ahead. Don't look further than that, because you are not to waste energy unnecessarily.

When you look, you are throwing out a certain amount of energy. Wait, be silent, allow that energy to come back, and you will be surprised. If you can allow the energy to come back, you will never feel exhausted. Do it. Tomorrow morning, try it. Be silent, look at something. Be silent, don't think about it, and wait patiently for a single moment – the energy will come back; in fact, you may be revitalized.

Without thought, the energy comes back; there is no barrier. And if you are there you reabsorb it, this reabsorption is rejuvenating. Rather than your eyes being tired they feel more relaxed, more vital, filled with more energy.

taking space

We all need a certain amount of space. Whenever people encroach on that space, our energy shrinks and we become quite panicky inside.

And that space is becoming smaller and smaller every day. The world is becoming too crowded. Everywhere – in the train, in the bus, in the theatre, on the street, in the shops, in the restaurants, in colleges, in schools – there is a huge crowd of people and the space necessary for the growth of the individual has disappeared. A deep stress has arisen in every human being. They call it the 'stress syndrome' and now it has become almost normal.

Everybody is stressed, but because it has become normal, people are not aware of it. It creates many sorts of inner illnesses; particularly tension-related types of diseases.

Watch people in the train standing side by side, almost being crushed by each other – shrunken, hard, frozen, not moving, because they are afraid. If they move, the energy moves, so they remain frozen as if they are dead, so they cannot feel the presence of the other. That's how bodies have become more and more deadened, insensitive.

You have to do something about it, otherwise it will create problems. There is something you can do whenever people are close and you feel the first sign of panic, fear and strain. Exhale deeply and throw the air out. Just feel that the whole stress is being

thrown out with the air. Then inhale deeply. Take in fresh air and feel that your chest, your inner passage is expanding. Just seven breaths will do, and suddenly you will see that there is no problem.

The most important thing is the idea that with the exhalation you are throwing out stress. Breathing can be used to invite many things, to throw out many things. It is the most vital part of you. It is you. So whatever you do to your breathing, you are doing to yourself. When you are peaceful, at ease, your breathing is different. Just by watching your breath you can know what kind of state is happening in your mind.

conscious tasting

We eat very unconsciously, automatically, robot-like. If taste is not lived and experienced, you are just stuffing yourself. Go slowly, and be aware of the taste. Do not just go on swallowing things. Taste them unhurriedly and become the taste. When you feel sweetness, become that sweetness. And then it can be felt all over the body – not just in the mouth, not just on the tongue, it can be felt all over the body, spreading in ripples.

Whatever you are eating, feel the taste and become the taste. With no taste, your senses will be deadened. They will become less and less sensitive. And with less sensitivity, you will not be able to feel your body and you will not be able to feel your feelings. Then you will just remain centred in the head.

When drinking water, feel the coolness. Close your eyes, drink it slowly, taste it. Feel the coolness and feel that you have become that coolness, because the coolness is being transferred to you from the water; it is becoming a part of your body. Your mouth is touching it, your tongue is touching it, and the coolness is transferred. Allow it to happen to the whole of your body. Allow its ripples to spread, and you will feel a coolness all over your body. In this way your sensitivity can grow, and you can become more alive and more fulfilled.

the inner smile

Whenever you are sitting and you have nothing to do, just relax your lower jaw and open the mouth just slightly. Start breathing from the mouth but not deeply. Just let the body breathe so it will be shallow, and become more and more shallow. And when you feel that the breathing has become very shallow and the mouth is open and your jaw is relaxed, your whole body will feel very relaxed.

In that moment, start feeling a smile – not on the face but all over your inner being. It is not a smile that comes on the lips – it is an existential smile that spreads inside.

There is no need to smile with the lips on the face – but just as if you are smiling from the belly; the belly is smiling. And it is a smile, not a laugh, so it is very, very soft, delicate, fragile, like a small rose flower opening in the belly, allowing its fragrance to spread all over the body.

Once you have known what this smile is you can remain happy for 24 hours. And whenever you feel that you are missing that happiness, just close your eyes and catch hold of that smile again and it will be there. And during the day you can catch hold of it as many times as you want. It is always there.

rise with the sun

just 15 minutes before the sun rises, when the sky is becoming a little lighter, just wait and watch as one waits for a beloved: so alert, so deeply awaiting, so hopeful and excited – and yet silent. And just let the sun rise and go on watching. No need to stare; you can blink your eyes. Have the feeling that something inside is also rising simultaneously.

When the sun comes up on the horizon, start feeling that it is just near the navel.

It comes up over there; and here, inside the navel, it comes up, comes up, slowly. The sun is rising there, and inside the navel an inner point of light is rising.

Just ten minutes will do. Then close your eyes.

When you first see the sun with open eyes it creates a negative, so when you close your eyes, you can see the sun dazzling inside.

And this is going to change you tremendously.

saying yes

Our basic attitude is 'No'. Why? Because when you say 'no' you feel you are somebody. The mother feels she is somebody – she can say no. The child is negated, the child's ego is hurt and the mother's ego is fulfilled. 'No' is ego fulfilling; it is food for the ego, which is why we train ourselves in saying no.

Go anywhere in life and you will find no-sayers everywhere because with 'no' you feel your authority – you are someone, you can say no. To say, 'Yes, Sir' makes you feel inferior; you feel that you are someone's subordinate, nobody. Only then do you say 'Yes, Sir'.

Yes is positive and no is negative.

Remember this: no is ego fulfilling; yes is the method to discover the self. No is strengthening the ego; yes is destroying it.

First find out whether you can say yes. If you cannot say yes, if it is impossible to say yes, only then say no.

Our normal method is first to say no; if it is impossible to say no, only then, with a defeated attitude, do we say yes.

Try it some day. Take a vow that for 24 hours you will try in every situation to start with yes. Look what deep relaxation it offers you. Just ordinary things! The child asks to go to the cinema. He will go; your 'no' means nothing. On the contrary, your 'no' becomes an invitation, your 'no' becomes an attraction, because while you are

strengthening your ego the child is also trying to strengthen his. He will try to go against your no, and he knows ways to make your no a yes, he knows how to transform it. He knows it needs just a little effort, insistence, and your no becomes yes.

For 24 hours, try in every way to start with yes. You will feel great difficulty because you will become aware: immediately the no comes first! In anything the no comes first – that has become the habit. Don't use it; use yes, and then see how the yes relaxed you.

letting go of restlessness

every night, sit in a chair and let your head fall back, relaxed and at rest. You can use a pillow so you are in a resting posture and there is no tension in the neck. Then release your lower jaw – just relax it so the mouth opens slightly – and start breathing from the mouth, not from the nose. But the breathing must not be changed, it has to be as it is – natural. The first few breaths will be a little erratic. By and by the breaths will settle down and the breathing will become very shallow. It will go in and out very lightly; that's how it should be. Keep the mouth open, eyes closed, and rest.

Then start feeling that your legs are becoming loose, as if they are being taken away from you, broken loose at the joints. Feel as if they are being taken away from you – they have been cut loose – and then start thinking that you are just the upper part. The legs are gone.

Then the hands: imagine that both hands are becoming loose and being taken away from you. You may even be able to hear a 'click' inside when they break away. You are no longer your hands; they are dead, taken away. Then just the torso remains.

Then start thinking about the head – that it is being taken away; you are being beheaded and the head has broken away. Then leave it loose: wherever it turns – right or left – you cannot do anything. Just leave it loose; it has been taken away.

That essential part will relax and the energy will start flowing...

Then you have just your torso. Feel that you are only this much – the chest and the belly, that's all.

Do this for at least 20 minutes and then go to sleep. This is to be done just before sleep. Do it for at least three weeks.

Your restlessness will settle. Taking these parts as separate, only the essential will remain, so your whole energy will move in the essential part. That essential part will relax and the energy will start flowing in your legs, in your hands and in your head again, this time in a more proportionate way.

staying in touch with the heart

feeling is real life. Thinking is phoney because thinking is always about; it is never the real thing. It is not thinking about the wine that can make you intoxicated, it is the wine. You can go on thinking about the wine, but just by thinking about the wine you will never become intoxicated. You will have to drink it, and the drinking happens through feeling.

Thinking is a pseudo activity, a substitute activity. It gives you a false sense of something happening, and nothing happens. So shift from thinking to feeling, and the

best way will be to start breathing from the heart.

In the day, as many times as you remember, just take a deep breath. Feel it hitting just in the middle of the chest. Feel as if the whole existence is pouring into you, into the place where your heart centre is. It differs with different people; ordinarily it is leaning to the right. It has nothing to do with the physical heart. It is a totally different thing; it belongs to the subtle body.

Breathe deeply, and whenever you do, do it at least five times with deep breaths. Take the breath in and fill the heart. Just feel it in the middle, that existence is pouring in through the heart. Vitality, life, the divine, nature – everything pouring in. Then exhale deeply, again from the heart, and feel you are pouring all that has been given to you back into the divine, into existence.

Do it many times in the day, but whenever you do it, take five breaths at once. That will help you to shift from the head to the heart.

You will become more and more sensitive, more and more aware of many things of which you have not been aware. You will smell more, you will taste more, you will touch more. You will see more, you will hear more; everything will become intense. So move from the head to the heart and all your senses will suddenly become luminous. You will start feeling life really throbbing in you, ready to jump and ready to flow.

...all your senses will suddenly become luminous.

the stop! exercise

Stop yourself, stop yourself completely... Just be present...

Start doing a very simple exercise at least six times a day. It takes only half a minute each time, which is three minutes a day. It is the shortest meditation in the world! But you have to do it suddenly – that's the whole point of it.

Walking on the street, suddenly you remember. Stop yourself, stop yourself completely, no movement.

Just be present for half a minute. Whatever the situation, stop completely and just be present to whatever is happening. The stop has to be done suddenly. Then start moving again. Do this six times a day. You can do it more often but not less; it will bring great opening.

If you just become present suddenly, the whole energy changes. The continuity that was going on in the mind stops. And it is so sudden that the mind cannot create a new thought so quickly. It takes time; the mind is stupid.

Anywhere, the moment you remember, just give a jerk to your whole being and stop. Not only will you become aware. Soon you will feel that others have become aware of your energy – that something has happened; something from the unknown is entering you.

breaking out of the box

feeling sad? Dance, or go and stand under the shower and see sadness disappearing from your body as the body heat disappears. Feel that with the water showering on you, the sadness is being removed just as perspiration and dust are removed from the body. See what happens.

Try to put the mind in such a situation that it cannot function in the old way.

Anything will do. In fact all the techniques that have been developed through the centuries are nothing but ways of trying to distract the mind from the old patterns.

For example, if you are feeling angry just take a few deep breaths. Inhale deeply and exhale deeply, just for two minutes, and then see where your anger is. You confuse the mind; it cannot correlate the two. 'Since when,' the mind starts asking, 'did anyone ever breathe deeply with anger? What is going on?'

So do anything but never repeat it; that's the point. Otherwise if each time you feel sad you take a shower, the mind will get into that habit. After three or four times, the mind learns, 'This is okay. You are sad; that's why you are taking a shower.' Then it becomes part and parcel of your sadness. No, never repeat it. Just go on puzzling the mind every time. Be innovative, be imaginative.

Your partner says something and you feel angry. Usually when this happens, you want to hit him or throw something at him.

This time, change: go and hug him! Give him a big kiss and puzzle him as well! Your mind will be puzzled and he will be puzzled. Suddenly things are no longer the same. Then you will see that the mind is a mechanism; that with the new, it is simply at a loss; it cannot cope with the new.

Open up the window and let a new breeze blow through.

just listening

listening is a deep participation between the body and the soul. And that's why it has been used as one of the most powerful methods for meditation ... because it bridges the two infinities: the material and the spiritual.

Whenever you are sitting, just listen to whatever is going on. There is a marketplace and there is a lot of noise and traffic; you can hear a train and a plane. Listen, without thinking in the mind that it is noisy. Listen as if you are listening to music, with sympathy, and suddenly you will see that the quality of the noise has changed. It is no longer distracting, no longer disturbing; on the contrary, it becomes very soothing. If listened to rightly, even the marketplace becomes a melody.

So, what you are listening to is not the point; the point is that you are listening, not just hearing.

Even if you are listening to something that you have never thought of as worth listening to, listen to it very cheerfully – as if you were listening to a Beethoven sonata – and suddenly you will see you have transformed the quality of it. It becomes beautiful.

pillar of energy

a certain silence immediately comes to you if you stand quietly. Try it in the corner of your room. Just in the corner, stand silently, not doing anything. Suddenly the energy also stands inside you. Sitting down, you will feel many disturbances in the mind because sitting is the posture of a thinker; standing, the energy flows like a pillar and is distributed equally all over the body. Standing is beautiful.

Try it because some of you will find it very, very beautiful. If you can stand for one hour it is just wonderful. Just by standing and not doing anything, not moving, you will find that something settles within you, becomes silent, the centring happens and you will feel yourself like a pillar of energy. The body disappears.

collapsing into silence

Whenever you have time, just collapse into silence, and that's exactly what I mean – collapse, as if you were a baby in your mother's womb.

Sit on your knees on the floor, and then by and by you will start feeling that you want to put your head on the floor; then put your head on the floor. Adopt the womb posture, as the child remains curled up in the mother's womb. And immediately you will feel that the silence is coming, the same silence that was there in the mother's womb.

Sitting in your bed, go under a blanket and curl up. And remain there … utterly still, doing nothing. A few thoughts will sometimes come – let them pass, be indifferent, not concerned at all. If they come, good, if they don't come, good. Don't fight, don't push them away. If you fight you will become disturbed. If you push them away they will become persistent; if you don't want them, they will be very stubborn about going.

Simply remain unconcerned; let them be there on the periphery, as if the traffic noise is there.

And it really is a traffic noise – the brain traffic of millions of cells communicating with each other and energy moving and electricity jumping from one cell to another cell. It is just the humming of a great machine, so let it be there. Become completely indifferent to it; it does not concern you, it is not your

...collapse, as if you were a baby in your mother's womb.

problem – somebody else's problem maybe, but not yours. What have you got to do with it?

And you will be surprised: moments will come when the noise will disappear, completely disappear, and you will be left all alone. In that all-aloneness you will find silence. A womb posture – just as if you are in a mother's womb and there is not much space so you curl up, and it is cold, so cover yourself with a blanket. It will become a perfect womb, warm and dark, and you will feel yourself very, very small. It will give you a great insight into your being.

enjoying the drama

this whole world is just like a drama, so don't take it too seriously. Seriousness will force you into trouble; you will get into trouble. Don't be serious about it. Nothing is serious; this whole world is just a drama. If you can look at it as a drama you will regain your original consciousness.

The dust gathers because you are so serious. That seriousness creates problems, and we are so serious that even while seeing a drama we gather dust.

Go to a cinema and look at the spectators. Don't look at the screen, forget the picture; don't look at the screen, just look at the spectators in the cinema. Someone will be weeping and tears will be rolling down, someone will be laughing, someone will be sexually excited. Just look at people. What are they doing? What is happening to them? And there is nothing on the screen, just pictures – pictures of light and shadow.

The screen is vacant. But why are they getting excited? They are weeping, crying, laughing. The picture is not just a picture; the film is not just a film. They have forgotten that it is just a story. They have taken it seriously. It has become alive, it is 'real'!

And this is happening everywhere, not only in cinemas. Look at the life that is all around you. What is it? Many people have lived on this earth. Where you are sitting, at least ten dead bodies are buried in that place, and they too were serious like you. Now they

Nothing is serious; this whole world is just a drama

are no more. Where have their lives gone? Where have their problems gone? They were fighting – fighting for a single inch of earth, and the earth is still there and they are no more.

And I am not saying that their problems were not problems. They were, as your problems are, problems. They were 'serious' – matters of life and death. But where are their problems? And if the whole of humanity disappeared one day, the earth would still be there, the trees would grow, the rivers would flow and the sun would rise, and the earth would not feel any absence nor wonder where humanity was.

Look at the expanse: look backwards, look forwards, look to all dimensions at what you are, what your life is. It looks like a long dream, and everything that you take so seriously this moment becomes irrelevant the next moment. You may not even remember it. Remember your first love, how serious it was. Life depended on it. Now you don't remember it at all, it is forgotten. And whatever you are thinking that your life depends on today will eventually be forgotten.

Life is a flux, nothing remains. It is like a moving image, everything changing into everything else. But in the moment you feel it is very serious, and you get disturbed.

In India, we have called this world not a creation of God, but a play, a game, a *leela*. This concept of 'leela' is beautiful, because creation seems serious. The Christian, the Jewish God is very serious. Even for a single disobedient act, Adam was thrown out of the Garden of Eden – and not only was he thrown out, but the whole of humanity was thrown out because of him. He was our father, and we are suffering because of him. God seems to be so serious: he should not be disobeyed or he will take revenge.

And the revenge has gone on for so long! The sin doesn't seem to be so serious. In fact, Adam committed it because of God's own foolishness. God the Father said to Adam, 'Don't go near the tree, the Tree of Knowledge, and don't eat its fruit.'

This prohibition became an invitation, and this is psychological. In that big garden, only that Tree of Knowledge became attractive. It was prohibited. Any psychologist can tell you that God committed an error. If the fruit of that tree was not to be eaten, it would have been better not to have talked about it at all. There would have been no possibility of Adam reaching that tree, and the whole of humanity would still be in the garden.

But this order, 'Don't eat,' created the trouble; this 'don't' created the whole trouble.

Because Adam disobeyed he was thrown out of heaven, and the revenge seems to have continued for such a long time. And Christians say Jesus was crucified just to redeem us – to redeem us from the sin that Adam committed. So the whole Christian concept of history hangs on two people – Adam and Jesus. Adam committed the sin, and Jesus suffered to redeem us from it and allowed himself to be crucified. He suffered so that Adam's sin could be forgiven.

But it doesn't seem that God has forgiven us yet. Jesus was crucified, but humanity goes on suffering in the same way.

The very concept of God as a father is ugly, serious.

The Indian concept is not of a creator. God is just a player; he is not serious. This is just a game. Rules are there, but the rules of a game. You need not be serious about them. Nothing is sin – only error, and you suffer because of error, not because God punishes you. You suffer if you don't follow the rules. God is not punishing you.

The whole concept of leela gives life a dramatic colour; it becomes a long drama. And the technique is based on this concept: if you are unhappy, you have taken it too seriously.

Don't try to find a way to be happy. Just change your attitude. You cannot be happy with a serious mind. With a festive mind, you can be happy. Take this whole life as a myth, as a story. It is, and once you take it this way you will not be unhappy. Unhappiness comes out of too much seriousness.

For seven days take everything as a drama, just as a show.

Try for seven days; for seven days remember only one thing – that the whole world is just a drama – and you will not be the same again. Just for seven days! You are not going to lose much because you don't have anything to lose. You can try it. For seven days take everything as a drama, just as a show.

These seven days will give you many glimpses of your buddha nature, of your inner purity. And once you have had a glimpse, you will not be the same again.

You will be happy, and you cannot conceive of what type of happiness can happen to you because you have not known any happiness. You have known only degrees of unhappiness: sometimes you were more unhappy, sometimes less unhappy, and when you were less unhappy you called it happiness. You don't know what happiness is because you cannot know.

When you take the world very seriously, you cannot know what happiness is. Happiness happens only when you are grounded in the attitude that the world is just a play. So try this, and do everything in a very festive way, celebrating, doing an 'act' – not the real thing. If you are a husband, play, be a play husband; if you are a wife, be a play wife. Make it just a game.

And there are rules, of course; any game to be played needs rules. Marriage has its rules and divorce has its rules, but don't be serious about them. They are rules, and one rule begets another. Divorce is bad because marriage is bad: one rule begets another! But don't take them seriously, and then look at how the quality of your life immediately changes.

Go home this evening, and behave with your husband or your children as if you are playing a part in a drama, and see the beauty of it. If you are playing a part you will try to be efficient, but you will not get disturbed. There is no need. You will do the part and go to sleep. But remember, it is a part, and for seven days continuously maintain this attitude. Then happiness can come to you, and once you know what happiness is you need not move into unhappiness, because it is your choice.

You are unhappy because you have chosen a wrong attitude towards life. You can be happy if you choose a right attitude. Buddha makes it a base, a foundation – 'right attitude'. What is right attitude? What is the criterion? To me this is the criterion: the attitude that makes you happy is the right attitude, and there is no objective criterion. The attitude that makes you unhappy and miserable is the wrong attitude. The criterion is subjective; your happiness is the criterion.

complete the circle — a mirror meditation

Your consciousness is flowing outwards – this is a fact, not a question of belief. When you look at an object, your consciousness flows towards the object.

For example, you are looking at me. Then you forget yourself, you become focused on me. Then your energy flows towards me, then your eyes are arrowed towards me. This is extroversion. You see a flower and you are enchanted, and you become focused on the flower. You become oblivious of yourself, you are only attentive to the beauty of the flower.

This we know – every moment it happens. A beautiful woman passes by and suddenly your energy starts following her. We know this outward flow of light. This is only half of the story. But each time the light flows out, you fall into the background, you become oblivious of yourself.

The light has to flow back so that you are both the subject and the object at the same time, simultaneously, so that you see yourself.

Then self-knowledge is released. Ordinarily, we live only in this half way – half-alive, half-dead, that's the situation. And slowly, slowly light goes on flowing outwards and never returns. You see this, you see that, you are continuously seeing without ever returning the energy to the seer. In the day you see the world, in the night you see dreams, but you go on remaining constantly attached to objects. This is dissipating energy.

The Taoist experience is that this energy that you spend in your extroversion can be more and more crystallized rather than spent if you learn the secret science of turning it backwards. It is possible; that is the whole science of all methods of concentration.

Just standing before a mirror one day, try a small experiment. You are looking at the mirror, your own face in the mirror, your own eyes in the mirror. Then, for a moment, reverse the whole process. Start feeling that you are being looked at by the reflection in the mirror – not that you are looking at the reflection but that the reflection is looking at you – and you will be in a very strange space. And although it is not mentioned in Taoist scriptures this seems to me the most simple experiment anybody can do, and very easily. Just standing before the mirror in your bathroom, first look into the reflection: you are looking and the reflection is the object. This is extroversion: you are looking into the mirrored face – your own face, of course, but it is an object outside you. Then change the whole situation, reverse the process.

...look at the rose flower ... the rose flower is looking at you.

Start feeling that you are the reflection and the reflection is looking at you. And immediately you will see a change happening, a great energy moving towards you. Just try it for a few minutes and you will be very alive, and something of immense power will start entering you. You may even become frightened because you have never known it; you have never seen the complete circle of energy.

In the beginning it may be frightening because you have never done it and you have never known it; it will look crazy. You may feel shaken, a trembling may arise in you, or you may feel disoriented, because your whole orientation up to now has been extroversion. Introversion has to be learned slowly. But the circle is complete. And if you do it for a few days you will be surprised how much more alive you feel the whole day – just a few minutes standing before the mirror and letting the energy come back to you so the circle is complete. And whenever the circle is complete there is a great silence. The incomplete circle creates restlessness. When the circle is complete it creates rest, it makes you centred. And to be centred is to be powerful – the power is yours. And this is just an experiment; then you can try it in many ways.

Looking at the rose flower, first look at the rose flower for a few moments, a few minutes, and then start the reverse process: the rose flower is looking at you. And you will be surprised how much energy the rose flower can give to you. And the same can be done with trees and the stars and with people. And the best way is to do it with the woman or man you love. Just look into each other's eyes. First begin looking at the other and then start feeling the other returning the energy to you; the gift is coming back. You will feel replenished, you will feel showered, bathed, basked in a new kind of energy. You will come out of it rejuvenated, revitalized.

move from the head to the heart

try to be headless. Visualize yourself as headless; move headlessly. It sounds absurd, but it is one of the most important exercises. Try it, and then you will know. Walk, and feel as if you have no head. In the beginning it will be only 'as if'. It will be very weird. When the feeling comes to you that you have no head, it will be very weird and strange. But by and by you will settle down at the heart.

There is one law ... You may have seen that someone who is blind has keener ears, more musical ears. Blind people are more musical; their feeling for music is deeper. Why? The energy that ordinarily moves through the eyes now cannot move through them, so it chooses a different path. It moves through the ears.

Blind people have a deeper sensitivity of touch. If a blind person touches you, you will feel the difference, because we ordinarily do much work with touch through our eyes; we are touching each other through our eyes. A blind person cannot touch through the eyes, so the energy moves through the hands. A blind person is more sensitive than anyone who has eyes. Sometimes it may not be so, but generally it is so. Energy starts moving from another centre if one centre is not there.

So try this exercise in headlessness – and suddenly you will feel a strange thing: it will be as if for the first time you are at the heart. Walk headlessly. Sit down to meditate, close

your eyes, and simply feel that there is no head. Feel, 'My head has disappeared.' In the beginning it will be just 'as if', but by and by you will feel that the head has really disappeared. And when you feel that your head has disappeared, your centre will fall down to the heart – immediately. You will be looking at the world through the heart and not through the head.

When for the first time Westerners reached Japan, they couldn't accept that the Japanese had traditionally believed for centuries that people think through the belly. If you ask a Japanese child – if he is not educated in Western ways – 'Where is your thinking?' he will point to his belly.

Centuries and centuries have passed, and Japan has been living without the head. It is just a concept. If I ask you, 'Where is your thinking going on?', you will point towards the head, but a Japanese person will point to the belly, not to the head. And one of the reasons why the Japanese mind is more calm, quiet and collected, is this.

Now this concept has been disturbed because the West has spread over everything. Now there exists no East. Only in some individuals here and there, that are like islands, does the East exist. Otherwise the East has disappeared; now the whole world is Western.

Try headlessness. Meditate standing before your mirror in the bathroom. Look deep into your eyes and feel that you are looking from the heart. By and by the heart centre will begin to function. And when the heart

functions, it changes your total personality, the total structure, the whole pattern, because the heart has its own way.

So the first thing: try headlessness. Secondly, be more loving, because love cannot function through the head. Be more loving! That is why when someone is in love, she loses her head. People say that she has gone mad. If you are not mad and in love, then you are not really in love. The head must be lost. If the head is there, unaffected, functioning ordinarily, then love is not

possible, because for love you need the heart to function – not the head. It is a function of the heart.

It happens that when a very rational person falls in love, he becomes stupid. He himself feels what stupidity he is indulging in, what silliness. What is he doing? Then he makes two parts of his life. He creates a division. The heart becomes a silent, intimate affair. When he moves out of his house, he moves out of his heart. He lives in the world with the head, and only comes down to the

heart when he is loving. But it is very difficult, and ordinarily it never happens.

I was staying in Bombay at a friend's house, and the friend was a senior police officer. His wife told me, 'I have only one problem to tell you about. Can you help me?'

So I said, 'What is the problem?'

She said, 'My husband is your friend. He loves you and respects you, so if you say something to him it may be helpful.'

So I asked her, 'What is to be said? Tell me.' She said, 'He remains a senior police officer even in bed. I have not known a lover, a friend or a husband. He is a senior police officer 24 hours a day.'

It is difficult, it is difficult to come down from your pedestal. It becomes a fixed attitude. If you are a businessman, you will remain a businessman in bed too. It is difficult to accommodate two persons within, and it is not easy to change your pattern completely, immediately, any time you like. It is difficult, but if you are in love you will have to come down from the head.

So for this meditation try to be more and more loving. And when I say be more loving, I mean change the quality of your relationship: let it be based on love. Not only with your wife or with your child or with your friend, but towards life as such become more loving. That is why Mahavir and Buddha have talked about non-violence. It was just to create a loving attitude towards life.

When Mahavir moves, walks, he remains aware not to kill even an ant. Why? Really, the ant is not his concern. He is coming down

Touch your food lovingly, with gratitude: it is your life.

from the head to the heart. He is creating a loving attitude towards life as such. The more your relationships are based on love – all relationships – the more your heart centre will function. It will start working; you will look at the world through different eyes, because the heart has its own way of looking at the world. The mind can never look in that way – that is impossible for the mind. The mind can only analyse! The heart synthesizes; the mind can only dissect, divide – it is a divider. Only the heart gives unity.

When you can look through the heart, the whole universe looks like one unity. When you approach through the mind, the whole world becomes atomic. There is no unity, only atoms and more atoms. The heart gives a unitary experience, it joins together, and the ultimate synthesis is God. If you can look through the heart, the whole universe looks like one. That oneness is God.

That is why science can never find God. That is impossible, because the method applied can never reach to the ultimate unity. The very method of science is reason, analysis, division. So science comes down to molecules, atoms, electrons. Scientists will go on dividing, but they can never come to the organic unity of the whole. The whole is impossible to look at through the head.

So be more loving. Remember, whatever you are doing, the quality of love must be there. This has to be a constant remembering. You are walking on the grass – feel that the grass is alive. Every blade is as much alive as you are.

Be loving. Even with things, be loving. If you are sitting on a chair, be loving. Feel the chair; have a feeling of gratitude. The chair is giving comfort to you. Feel the touch, love it, have a loving feeling. The chair itself is not important. If you are eating, eat lovingly.

Indians say that food is divine. The meaning is that when you are eating, the food is giving you life, energy, vitality. Be grateful, be loving towards it.

Ordinarily we eat food very violently, as if we are killing something, not as if we are absorbing – as if we are killing. Or very indifferently you go on throwing things into your belly, without any feeling. Touch your food lovingly, with gratitude: it is your life. Take it in, taste it, enjoy it. Do not be indifferent and do not be violent.

Our teeth are very violent because of our animal heritage. Animals have no other weapons; nails and teeth are their only weapons of violence. Your teeth are basically a weapon, so people go on killing with their teeth – they kill their food. That is why, the more violent you are, the more you will need food.

But there is a limit to food, so one also smokes or chews gum. That is violence. You enjoy it because you are killing something with your teeth, grinding something with your teeth, so one goes on chewing gum. This is a part of violence. Do whatever you are doing, but do it lovingly. Do not be indifferent. Then your heart centre will start functioning, and you will come down deep into the heart.

air space for road warriors

You cannot find a better situation to meditate than while flying at a high altitude. The higher the altitude, the easier is the meditation. Hence, for centuries, meditators have been moving to the Himalayas to reach a high altitude.

When gravity is weaker and the earth is very far away, the many pulls of the earth are far away. You are far away from the corrupted society that humankind has built. You are surrounded by clouds and the stars and the moon and the sun and the vastness of space.

So do one thing: start feeling at one with that vastness, and do it in three steps.

The first step: for a few minutes just think that you are becoming bigger, and soon you will be able to feel that you have become bigger ... you are filling the whole cockpit.

Then the second step: start feeling that you are becoming even bigger, bigger than the plane, in fact the plane is now inside you.

And the third step: feel that you have expanded into the whole sky. Now these clouds that are moving on your radar screen, and the moon, and the stars – they are moving in you: you are huge, unlimited.

This feeling will become your meditation, and you will feel completely relaxed, no longer tense. Your work will become just child's play and it will not cause you any stress – it will happen of its own accord. You will arrive after the flight fresher than you had begun. And keep quiet. Tell people not to talk too much to you unless it is necessary. Or you can just put a sign on yourself saying 'I am meditating', so people know not to disturb you. It's great ... nothing like it!

In fact in the early days – when the aeroplane had just been invented – the thrill of the aeroplane was the thrill of the sky. But we go on losing sensations because they become too routine. Now that people fly almost every day, who looks at the sky and who looks at the sun making beautiful psychedelic colours on the clouds – who looks?

So start looking at the sky that surrounds you and by and by let there be a meeting between the inner sky and the outer sky.

The higher the altitude, the easier is the meditation.

part five

untying the knots – active meditations to find stillness within

Be so active that your whole energy starts moving, no energy is left static in you. All the frozen parts of your energy are melting, flowing. You are not a frozen thing now; you have become dynamic. You are not material; you have become electrical.

When everything is moving and you have become a cyclone, then become alert. Remember, be mindful – and in this cyclone suddenly you will find a centre that is absolutely silent. This is the centre of the cyclone. This is you – you in your divinity, you as a god.

All around you is activity. But just in the centre, amidst all this movement, there is a non-moving point, the still point. This still point has not to be created. It is already there! It has always been there. It is your very being, the very ground of your being.

why catharsis is helpful

body and mind function together. The mind is the inner aspect of the body – it is a material phenomenon, it has nothing to do with your being. It is matter as much as your body is, so if you do something with the body it automatically affects the mind. Hence down the ages, people have been cultivating postures – for example, sitting in a lotus posture, forcing the body to be like a statue, a marble statue. If your body is forced to be really still, you will see your mind fall into a kind of silence, which is false, which is not true. The body has just been forced by the body posture to be silent. Try it: just make the posture of anger with your fists, your face, your teeth; just go into the posture of anger and you will be surprised, you start feeling angry. That's what the actor does: she moves the body into the posture and the mind follows it.

Two great psychologists, James and Lange, discovered a very strange theory at the beginning of the 20th century. It is known as the James-Lange theory. They said something very unusual, which goes against the old common sense of the ages. Ordinarily we think that when a man is afraid he runs away; in fear, he starts running. James and Lange said it is not true – because he runs, that's why he feels fear.

It seems absurd, but it has some truth in it. The common-sense truth was half of the truth and this is the other half. If you start laughing, you will find yourself feeling a little less sad than you were before. You go and sit with a few friends who are laughing and telling jokes and you forget your sadness, your misery. You start laughing, and once you start laughing you feel good. You start with the body.

Try it! If you are feeling sad, start running, go running around the block seven times, breathing deep breaths, in the sun, in the wind; and after seven rounds, stand and see whether your mind is the same. No, it can't be the same. The bodily change has changed the mind.

The body chemistry changes the mind. Hence yoga postures – they are all postures to force the mind into a certain pattern. That is not real silence. The real silence has to be a silence that comes on its own. My suggestion is not to force your body. Rather, dance, sing, move, run, jog, swim. Let the body have all kinds of movement so your mind also has all kinds of movement, and through all those inner movements, the mind begins catharsis, and releases its poisons.

Shout, be angry, beat a pillow and you will be surprised – after beating a pillow you feel very good. Something in the mind has been released. It does not matter whether you were beating your boyfriend, your husband or the pillow. The pillow will do as perfectly well as the husband, because the body does not know whom you are beating. Just the very posture of beating, and the mind starts releasing its anger. Mind and body collaborate.

Start with catharsis, so that you become empty of all the rubbish that has been accumulating in you from your very childhood. You were angry but you could not be angry because the mother became mad if you became angry – so you repressed it. You were angry, you wanted to shout, but you could not shout; on the contrary, you smiled. All that is accumulated inside you – it has to be thrown out. And then wait ... and a silence starts descending on you. That silence has a beauty of its own. It is totally different; its quality is different, its depth is different.

gibberish meditation

You may not be sleeping well at night. Very few people sleep well, so when you have not slept well in the night you are a little tired during the day. If that is the case, then do something with your sleep. It should be made deeper. Time is not much of a question – you can sleep for eight hours but if it is not deep you will still feel hungry for sleep, starved – depth is the question.

Every night before you go to sleep try this little technique, which will help tremendously. Put the lights off, sit in your bed ready to sleep, but sit for 15 minutes. Close your eyes and then start any monotonous nonsense sound, for example: la, la, la – and wait for the mind to supply new sounds. The only thing to be remembered is that those sounds or words should not be of any language that you know. If you know English, German, Italian, then they should not be Italian, German or English. Any other language is allowed that you don't know – Tibetan, Chinese, Japanese. But if you know Japanese then it is not allowed, then Italian is wonderful.

Speak any language that you don't know. You will find this difficult for a few seconds on the first day, because how do you speak a language you don't know? It can be spoken, and once it starts, say any sounds, nonsense words, just to put the conscious off and allow the unconscious to speak ... When the

start the day with laughter

unconscious speaks, the unconscious knows no language.

It is a very, very old method. It comes from the Old Testament. It was called in those days *glossolalia* and a few churches still use it. They call it 'speaking in tongues'. And it is a wonderful method, one of the most deep and most penetrating into the unconscious. You start by saying 'la, la, la', and then you say anything that comes out. Just on the first day you will feel it is a little difficult. Once it comes, you have got the knack. Then for 15 minutes, use the language that is coming to you, and use it as a language, as if you are talking in it. This will relax the conscious very deeply.

Do this for 15 minutes, and then simply lie down and go to sleep. Your sleep will become deeper. Within weeks you will feel a depth in your sleep, and in the morning you will feel completely fresh.

When you get up, don't open your eyes first. When you feel the sleep is gone, just start laughing in your bed.

For the first two or three days it will be difficult, then it comes – and then it comes like an explosion. At first it is difficult because you feel foolish: why are you laughing? There is no reason. But by and by you will feel foolish and you will start laughing at your foolishness – and then it takes over. Then it is irrepressible. Then you laugh at the whole absurdity. And then somebody else – your wife, your girlfriend, the neighbour – may start laughing, seeing that you are a fool, and then that will help you. Laughter can become epidemic.

a centring device

You are already integrated. Not on the periphery – on the periphery there is much turmoil; you are fragmented on the periphery. Move inwards, and the deeper you go, the more you will find that you are integrated. There comes a point, at the very innermost shrine of your being, where you suddenly find you are a unity, an absolute unity. So it is a question of discovering it.

How do you discover it? There is a very simple technique, but in the beginning it looks very hard. If you try, you will find it is simple. If you don't try and only think about it, it will look very hard. The technique is to do only that which you enjoy. If you don't enjoy something, don't do it. Try it – because enjoyment comes only from your centre. If you are doing something and you enjoy it, you start getting reconnected with the centre. If you do something that you don't enjoy, you are disconnected from the centre. Joy arises from the centre and from nowhere else. So let it be a criterion, and be fanatical about it.

You are walking on the road; suddenly you realize that you are not enjoying the walk. Stop. Finished – this is not to be done.

I used to do it in my university days, and people thought that I was crazy. Suddenly I would stop, and then I would remain in that spot for half an hour, an hour, until I started enjoying walking again. If I was taking my bath and suddenly I realized that I was not enjoying it, I would stop – what is the point then? If I was eating and I realized suddenly that I was not enjoying it, then I would stop. My professors were so worried that when there were examinations they would put me in a car and take me to the university. They would leave me at the door of the hall and wait there to see if I had reached my desk or had stopped in the middle of the room. I joined the mathematics class in my high school. The first day, I went in and the teacher was just introducing the subject. In the middle I stood up and tried to walk out. He said, 'Where are you going? If you leave without asking, I won't allow you in again.' I said, 'I'm not coming back again; don't worry.

That's why I didn't ask. Finished – I am not
enjoying it! I will find some other subject that
I can enjoy, because if I cannot enjoy it I am
not going to do it. It is torture, it is violence.'

By and by, it became a key. I suddenly
realized that whenever you are enjoying
something, you are centred. Enjoyment is just
the sound of being centred. Whenever you are
not enjoying something, you are off centre. In
that case, don't force it; there is no need. If
people think you are crazy, let them think
you are crazy. Within a few days you will, by
your own experience, find out what you have
been missing. You were doing a thousand and
one things that you never enjoyed, and still
you were doing them because you were
taught to. You were just fulfilling your duties.

People have even destroyed such a
beautiful thing as love. You come home and
you kiss your husband because it has to be
so, it has to be done. Now, a beautiful thing
like a kiss, a flower-like thing, has been
destroyed. By and by, without enjoying it,
you will go on kissing your husband; you will
forget the joy of kissing another human
being. You shake hands with just anybody
you meet – cold, with no meaning in it, with
no message in it, no warmth flowing. Just
dead hands shaking each other and saying
'hello'. You learn this dead gesture, this cold
gesture. You become frozen, you become an
ice cube. And then you say, 'How do I get in
touch with my centre?'

The centre is available when you are warm, when you are flowing, melting, in love, in ecstasy, in dance, in delight. It is up to you. Just go on doing only those things that you really love to do and that you enjoy. If you don't enjoy something, stop doing it. Find something else that you enjoy. There is bound to be something that you will enjoy. I have never come across a person who cannot enjoy anything. There are people who may not enjoy one thing or another, but life is vast. Don't remain engaged, become floating. Let there be more streaming of energy. Let it flow, let it meet with other energies that surround you. Soon you will be able to see that the problem was not how to become integrated, the problem was that you have forgotten how to flow. In flowing energy, you are suddenly integrated. It sometimes happens accidentally, but for the same reason.

Sometimes you fall in love with a woman or a man, and suddenly you feel integrated; suddenly you feel you are one for the first time. Your eyes have a glow, your face has a radiance and your intellect is no longer dull. Something starts burning bright in your being – a song arises, your walk has a quality of dance in it now. You are a totally different being.

But these are rare moments, because we don't learn the secret. The secret is that there is something that you have started to enjoy. That's the whole secret. A painter may be hungry and painting, and still you can see that his face is so contented. A poet may be poor, but when he is singing his song he is the richest man in the world. Nobody is richer than he is. What is the secret of it? The secret is that he is enjoying this moment. Whenever you enjoy something, you are in tune with yourself and you are in tune with the universe – because your centre is the centre of all.

So let this small insight be a key for you. Do only what you enjoy, otherwise stop. If you are reading a newspaper and halfway through it you suddenly realize that you are not enjoying it, then there is no point. Why are you reading it? Stop immediately. If you are talking to somebody and in the middle of the conversation you realize that you are not enjoying it, even if you have said just half a sentence, stop there and then. You are not enjoying it so you are not obliged to continue. In the beginning it will look a little weird. But everybody is a little weird, so I don't think this is a problem. You can practise it.

Within a few days you will make many contacts with your centre, and then you will understand what I mean when I go on repeating again and again that that which you are seeking is already within you. It is not in the future. It has nothing to do with the future. It is already here now; it is already the case.

running, jogging and swimming

It is natural and easy to keep alert while you are in movement. When you are just sitting silently, the natural thing is to just fall asleep. When you are lying on your bed it is very difficult to keep alert because the whole situation leads you to fall asleep. But in movement naturally you cannot fall asleep, you function in a more alert way. The only problem is that the movement can become mechanical.

Learn to melt your body, mind and soul. Find ways in which you can function as a unity.

It happens many times to runners. You might not think of running as a meditation, but runners have sometimes felt a tremendous experience of meditation. And they were surprised, because they were not looking for it – who thinks that a runner is going to experience God? But it has happened. And now, more and more, running is becoming a new kind of meditation. It can happen in running.

If you have ever been a runner, if you have enjoyed running in the early morning when the air is fresh and young and the whole world is coming back from sleep, awakening ... you were running and your body was functioning beautifully, the fresh air, the new world born again out of the darkness of the night, everything singing all around, you were feeling so alive ... a moment comes when the runner disappears, and there is only running. The body, mind and soul start functioning together; suddenly an inner orgasm is released.

Sometimes, runners accidentally experience a state where the mind disappears and only pure awareness remains, although they tend to miss it. They will think it was just because of running that they enjoyed the moment: that it was a beautiful day, the body was healthy and the world was beautiful, and it was just a certain mood. They will generally not take any notice of it, but they may do. My own observation is that a runner can come close to meditation more easily than anybody else.

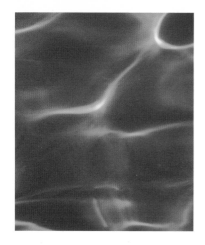 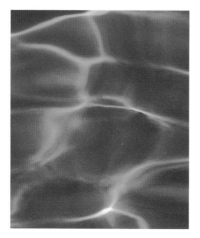 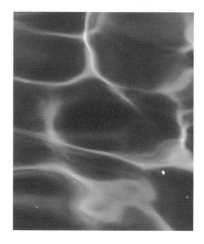

...rest, perspire and let the cool breeze come; feel peaceful.

Jogging can be of immense help, swimming can be of immense help. All these things have to be transformed into meditations.

Drop the old idea of meditation, that just sitting underneath a tree in a yoga posture is meditation. That is only one of the ways, and it may be suitable for a few people but it is not suitable for all. For a small child it is not meditation, it is torture. For a young man who is alive and vibrant it is repression, it is not meditation.

Start running in the morning on the road. Start with half a kilometre and then one kilometre and eventually try to run at least five kilometres. While running use the whole body; don't run as if you are in a straitjacket. Run like a small child, using the whole body – hands and feet – and run. Breathe deeply and from the belly. Then sit under a tree, rest, perspire and let the cool breeze come; feel peaceful. This will help greatly.

Sometimes just stand on the earth without shoes and feel the coolness, the softness, the warmth. Whatever the earth is ready to give in that moment, just feel it and let it flow through you. And allow your energy to flow into the earth. Be connected with the earth.

If you are connected with the earth, you are connected with life. If you are connected with the earth, you are connected with your body. If you are connected with the earth, you will become very sensitive and centred, and that's what is needed.

Never become an expert in running; remain an amateur so that alertness may be maintained. If you feel sometimes that running has become automatic, drop it; try swimming. If that becomes automatic, then try dancing. The point to remember is that the movement is just a situation to create awareness. While it creates awareness it is good. If it stops creating awareness, then it is no longer of any use; change to another movement during which you will have to be alert again. Never allow any activity to become automatic.

osho® nadabrahma meditation

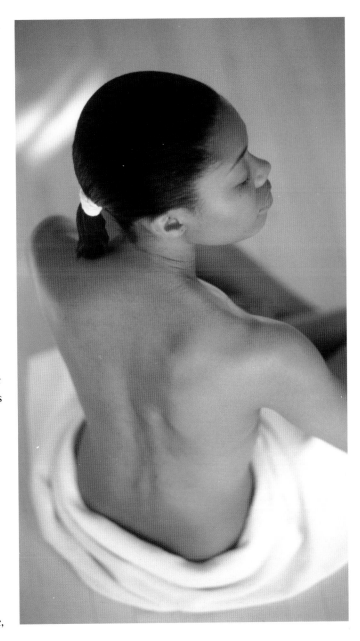

nadabrahma is a mantra meditation. It is very simple yet tremendously effective, because when you chant a mantra or you chant a sound, your body starts vibrating; your brain cells in particular start vibrating.

If done rightly your whole brain becomes tremendously vibrant, and the whole body also. Once the body starts vibrating and your mind is already chanting, they both fall in a tune. There is a harmony – which is ordinarily never there – between the two. Your mind goes on its way, your body continues on its own. The body goes on eating, the mind goes on thinking, the body goes on walking on the road, the mind is moving far away up in the stars. The mind and body never meet – they go on separate pathways, and that creates a split.

This basic schizophrenia is created because the body goes in one direction, the mind goes in another direction. And you are the third element – you are neither the body nor the mind, so you are pulled apart by these two. Half of your being is pulled by the body and half of your being is pulled by your mind. So there is great anguish – one feels torn apart.

In a mantra meditation – nadabrahma or any kind of chanting – this is how the mechanism works. When you start chanting a sound – and any sound will do; even 'abracadabra' – if you start resounding inside,

the body starts responding. Sooner or later a moment comes when the body and the mind move together in the same direction for the first time. When body and mind are both together, you are free from the body and the mind – you are not torn apart. Then the third element that you are in reality – call it soul, spirit, atma, anything – that third element is at ease because it is not being pulled in different directions.

The body and the mind are so much engrossed in chanting that the soul can slip out of them very easily, unobserved, and can become a witness; it can stand out and look at the whole game that is going on between the mind and the body. It is such a beautiful rhythm that the mind and body never become aware that the soul has slipped out, because they don't allow it so easily, do they? They want to hold on to their possession. Nobody wants to lose his possession. The body wants to dominate the soul and the mind wants to dominate the soul.

This is a very sly way to escape from their grip. They become drunk with the chanting, and you slip out!

So in the Nadabrahma Meditation, remember this: let the body and mind be totally together, but remember that you have to become a witness. Get away from them, easily, slowly, out of the back door, with no fight, with no struggle. They are drinking – you get out, and watch from the outside.

This is the meaning of the English word ecstasy – to stand outside. Stand outside and watch from there … and it is tremendously peaceful. It is silence, it is bliss, it is benediction.

This is the whole secret of chanting – that's why chanting has prevailed down the centuries. There has never been a religion that has not used chanting and mantra. But there is a danger also! If you don't get out, if you don't become a witness, there is a danger that you have missed the whole point. If you become drunk with the body and the mind and your soul also becomes drunk, then chanting is an intoxicant. Then it is like a tranquillizer – it will bring you good sleep, that's all. It is a lullaby. Good – nothing wrong with it – but not of any real value either.

So this is the pitfall to be remembered: chanting is so beautiful that one wants to get lost. If you are lost, then this is fine, you enjoyed a rhythm, an inner rhythm, and it was beautiful and you liked it, but it was like a drug – it was like an acid trip. By chanting, by the sound, you created certain drugs in your body.

Chanting creates chemical changes in the body, and those changes are no different from those created by marijuana or LSD. Some day, when research goes deeper into meditation, they are going to find that chanting creates chemical changes, just as fasting also creates chemical changes.

After the seventh or eighth day of fasting, one feels tremendously jubilant, weightless, very glad for no reason, delighted – as if all burdens have disappeared. Your body has created a certain chemical change.

I am as much against LSD as I am against fasting. And if chanting is used as a drug, I am against it. So the point to be remembered is that you should not use the sound, the chanting, the mantra as an intoxicant for your being. Let it be an intoxicant for the body and the mind but make sure that you slip out of it before you become intoxicated; you should stand outside and watch. You see the body swaying and you see the mind feeling very, very peaceful and calm and quiet. Watch from the outside and be alert like a flame.

If this is not done you will sleep well but nothing more. Then it is a good thing for your health but does nothing for your ultimate growth. So remember to slip out of it. Let the body get drunk, let the mind get drunk, let them fall into a deep love affair with each other, and then slip out of it. Don't stay there any longer, otherwise you will fall asleep. And if one falls asleep, it is not meditation. Meditation means awareness. So remember this!

nadabrahma meditation instructions

nadabrahma is an old Tibetan technique, which was originally performed in the early hours of the morning. It can be done at any time of the day, alone or with others, but make sure to have an empty stomach and remain inactive for at least 15 minutes afterwards. The meditation lasts an hour, and there are three stages.

First stage • 30 minutes

Sit in a relaxed position with eyes closed and lips together. Start humming, loudly enough to be heard by others and create a vibration throughout your body. You can visualize a hollow tube or an empty vessel, filled only with the vibrations of the humming. A point will come when the humming continues by itself and you become the listener. There is no special breathing and you can alter the pitch or move your body smoothly and slowly if you feel it.

Second stage • 15 minutes

The second stage is divided into two 7½-minute sections. For the first half, move the hands, palms up, in an outward circular motion. Starting at the navel, both hands move forwards and then divide to make two large circles mirroring each other left and right. The movement should be so slow that at times there will appear to be no movement at all. Feel that you are giving energy outwards to the universe.

After 7½ minutes turn the hands palms down, and start moving them in the opposite direction. Now the hands will come together towards the navel and divide outwards to the sides of the body. Feel that you are taking energy in. As in the first stage, don't inhibit any soft, slow movements of the rest of your body.

Third stage • 15 minutes

Sit or lie absolutely quiet and still.

nadabrahma for couples

artners sit facing each other, covered by a bedsheet and holding each other's crossed hands. It is best to wear no other covering. Light the room only with four small candles and burn a special incense, kept only for this meditation.

Close your eyes and hum together for 30 minutes. After a short while the energies will be felt to meet, merge and unite.

afterword

Start being aware with day-to-day, routine actions, and while you are doing your routine actions, remain relaxed. There is no need to be tense. When you are washing the floor, what is the need to be tense? Or when you are cooking food, what is the need to be tense? There is not a single thing in life that requires your tension. It is just your unawareness and your impatience.

I have lived in all kinds of ways, with all kinds of people. And I have always been puzzled: why are they tense?

It seems tension has nothing to do with anything outside you, it has something to do with what is within you. Outside you always find an excuse only because it looks so idiotic to be tense without any reason. In order to rationalize it, you find some reason outside yourself to explain why you are tense.

But tension is not outside of you, it lies in your incorrect lifestyle. You are living in competition – that will create tension. You are living in continuous comparison – that will create tension. You are always thinking either of the past or of the future, and missing the present, which is the only reality – that will create tension.

It is a question of simple understanding. There is no need to compete with anybody. You are yourself, and as you are, you are perfectly good.

Accept yourself.

This is the way existence wants you to be. Some trees are taller; some trees are smaller. But the smaller trees are not tense; neither are the taller trees full of ego. Existence needs variety. Somebody is stronger than you; somebody is more intelligent than you – but in some other way, you will be more talented than anybody else.

Just find your own talent. Nature never sends any single individual without some unique gift. Just search a little. Perhaps you can play the flute better than the president of the country can be a president – you are a better flautist than he is a president.

There is no question of any comparison. Comparison leads people astray. Competition keeps them continuously tense, and because their life is empty, they never live for the moment. All they do is think of the past, which is no more, or project into the future, which is not yet.

This whole thing drives people almost insane. There is no need; no animal goes mad, no tree needs psychoanalysis. The whole of existence is living in constant celebration, except human beings. They are sitting aloof, tense, worried.

A small life, and you are losing it and every day death is coming closer. That creates even more angst – 'death is coming closer and I have not even started living.' Most people realize only when they die that they were alive – but then it is too late.

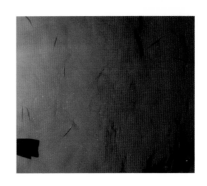

You are yourself, and as you are, you are perfectly good. Accept yourself.

Just live the moment.

And whatever qualities and whatever talents you have, use them to the fullest.

One of the mystics in India, Kabir, was a weaver. He had thousands of followers and still he continued to weave clothes. Even kings were his followers. The king of Varanasi asked him, 'Master, it doesn't look good, it makes us feel embarrassed. We can take care of you. There is no need for you to weave clothes and go to the market every week on market day, to sell your clothes. Just think of us! People think we are not taking care of you.'

Kabir said, 'I can understand your problem but I have only one talent and that is to weave beautiful clothes. If I stop doing it, who will do it? And God comes in different faces, in different bodies, to purchase clothes every week in the marketplace.'

He used to address every customer: 'Lord, be very careful with the cloth. I have been weaving it not just like any other weaver – my songs are in it and my soul is in it. I have poured my whole being into it. Be careful, use it with tenderness and love and remember: Kabir has woven it especially for you, Lord.' And it was not something that he said only to some people, he said it to all his customers.

This was his contribution. He used to say to his disciples, 'What else can I do? I am doing my best: I can weave, I can sing, I can dance, and I am immensely contented.'

Whatever you are doing, if you are content and feel that this whole existence is nothing but the manifestation of godliness, that we are travelling on holy earth, that whoever you are meeting, you are meeting God ... if you feel that there is no other way – only faces are different, but the inner reality is the same – all your tensions will disappear. And the energy that is involved in tension will start becoming your grace, your beauty.

Then life will not be just an ordinary, routine, day-to-day existence, but a dance from cradle to grave. And existence will be immensely enriched by your grace, by your relaxation, by your silence, by your awareness. You will not leave the world without contributing something valuable to it.

But people are always looking at others, at what others are doing – somebody is playing the flute and you cannot, and immediately there is misery; somebody is painting and you cannot, and there is misery.

Whatever you are doing, do it with such love, with such care that the smallest thing in the world becomes a work of art. It will bring great joy to you. And it will create a world without competition, without comparison; it will give dignity to all people; it will restore their pride.

Any act done with totality becomes your prayer.

further information

About the Author

Osho's teachings defy categorization, covering everything from the individual quest for meaning to the most urgent social and political issues facing society today. His books are not written but are transcribed from audio and video recordings of extemporaneous talks given to international audiences over a period of 35 years.

Osho characterizes his work as helping to create the conditions for the birth of a new kind of human being. He has often characterized this new human being as 'Zorba the Buddha' – a person capable both of enjoying the earthy pleasures of a Zorba the Greek and the silent serenity of a Gautama Buddha.

Running like a thread through all aspects of Osho's teachings is a vision that encompasses both the timeless wisdom of the East and the highest potential of Western science and technology.

Osho is also known for his revolutionary contribution to the science of inner transformation, with an approach to meditation that acknowledges the accelerated pace of contemporary life. His unique 'Active Meditations' are designed to first release the accumulated stresses of body and mind, so that it is easier to experience the thought-free and relaxed state of meditation.

OSHO® Meditation Resort

This is a place where people can have a direct personal experience of a new way of living with more alertness, relaxation and fun. Located southeast of Mumbai in Pune, India, the resort offers a variety of programmes to thousands of visitors each year from around the world. All resort programmes are based in the Osho vision of a qualitatively new kind of human being who is able both to participate creatively in everyday life and to relax into silence and meditation. Most programmes take place in modern, air-conditioned facilities and include a variety of individual sessions, courses and workshops covering everything from creative arts to holistic health treatments, personal transformation and therapy, esoteric sciences, the 'Zen' approach to sports and recreation, relationship issues and significant life transitions for men and women. For programme details and travel information see *www.osho.com/resort*

Websites

www.osho.com

A comprehensive website that includes video instruction for OSHO® Active Meditations, a Frequently Asked Questions page, and details about special music CDs to accompany these meditations.

index

acknowledgements

Picture credits

Corbis: pp 9 Cameron, 10-11 Galen Rowell, 19 Philip Bailey, 21 Randy Faris, 26 Firefly Productions, 33 Peter Reynolds/Frank Lane Picture Agency, 35 Kennan Ward, 40-41 Catherine Wessel, 66 Terry Weggers, 75 Mark M. Lawrence, 77-78 Lindsay Hebberd 80-81, Patrick Giardino 82, Michael Prince, 84 Robert Landau, 93 Laureen March, 96-97 L.Clarke, 128 Tom Galliher, 128 Tom Galliher, 129 Herrmann/ Starke, 133 Michael Keller, 137 Juttaklee, 140 Robert Essel/NYC.

Getty-Images/Stone: pp 6-7 Matthew Antrobus, 12 Gerben Oppermans, 16 Judith Haeusler, 27 Richard Elliott, 28 Manfred Rutz, 60 Jana Leon, 68 Daly & Newton, 90-91 Tom Stock, 95 Ray Kachatorian, 101 Steve Taylor, 105 Markus Amon, 106 Jack Louth, 110 Luc Beziat, 118 Anthony Marsland, 124 Jim Franco, 127 Richard Ross, 139 A Witte/ C.Mahaney.

Getty-Images/Taxi: pp 24 Lisa Romerein, 36 David Sacks, 46 Charly Franklin, 48-49 Thayer Syme, 88 Michael Krasowitz, 100 Ken Reid, 107 Geoff du Feu, 112 Christoph Wilhelm, 125 David Norton.

Getty-Images/The Image Bank: pp 2 Regine M, 4 Shaun Egan, 18 Serge Krouglikoff, 38 Michael Melford, 43 Terie Rakke, 52 Ken Kochen, 58 Shuji Kobayashi, 70-71 Hans Neleman, 85 Ghislaine and Marie David de Lossy, 98 Leo Mason, 102 Amy Neunsinger, 108-109 John and Lisa Merrill, 113 Stuart Westmorland, 115 Tierry Dosogne, 131 Tom Bean, 134 Pete Turner.

Octopus Publishing Group Limited/Jerry Harpur 34/Andrew Lawson 79, 87/David Loftus 50/Peter Myers 29, 76, 122-123/Peter Pugh-Cook 56/William Reavell 103/Ian Wallace 57, 92/Mark Winwood 86, 114 top, 114 bottom, 126, 126-127/Jacqui Wornell 5, 20, 73/George Wright 67

Photodisc/Getty Images 53, 99

Publisher's Acknowledgements

Executive Editor: David Alexander
Managing Editor: Clare Churly
Creative Director Tracy Killick
Production Manager: Louise Hall

Designed and produced for Hamlyn by The Bridgewater Book Company

Creative Director: Terry Jeavons
Editorial Director: Jason Hook
Project designers: Anna Hunter-Downing, Lisa McCormick
Page make-up: Kevin Knight
Editors: Hazel Songhurst, Cath Senker
Picture Researcher: Vanessa Fletcher